To study the effect of mass-me
etc. on the psychologic:

By : Singh, Bhanwar

To study the effect of mass-media, TV, Internet and video games etc. on the physical development of children

By: Singh, Bhavna

CHAPTER-1

INTRODUCTION

The influence of the media on the psychosocial development of children is profound. Thus, it is important to discuss with parents their child's exposure to media and to provide guidance on age-appropriate use of all media, including television, radio, music, video games and the Internet. For last few years it has been observed that children are spending more time watching programmed on TV, interacting on social networking site using internet, and playing video games and it is affecting their. New a days children and adolescents spend an average of 3-5 hours per day with a variety of mass-media, including television, radio, videos, videogames, and the Internet.. Publicists, promoters, and sales personnel have at some point used all of these media to advocate what people should wear, what they should eat, and what values they should hold. Vivid colors and language tell us what is happening in the world and how to react to the events shown. Although much of our society's media seems dominated by superficial chitchat, hyped news events, and depictions of violence, it is also a source of education, humor, and nonviolent entertainment. Just remember that the effect of media will vary
with a child's age and stage of development.

Download Article

Most realize that although the different media forms can be used elegantly for mediated learning, their major objectives are entertainment and product promotion. In the following section, we discuss what we broadly term the entertainment industry in its role as a general, society-wide influence on young children. We first discuss two of its primary forms, print and television, and then treat other current media under the rubric of the industry in general.

Mass media is communication that is to a large group, or groups, of people in a short time (Mass Media, 2013,). This can be written, spoken or broadcast communication. Some of the most popular forms of mass media are newspapers, magazines, radio, advertisements, social media, television, Internet, and films/movies. Mass communication refers to the technology that is used to communicate to a large group, or groups of people in a short time frame (Pavlik & McIntosh, 2004). There are other forms of communication. Interpersonal communication is kind of how it sounds. It's more personal and is usually face-to-face between two or more people (Interpersonal Communication Skills, 2013,). Now, there can be interpersonal communication that is not face-to-face. For instance four individuals may have to work on a group project for school. They may choose to Face time one another. Face time is an application (or app) that people use for video conferencing/chatting using the Internet. Everyone will be able to see one another as they disclose information about their project, but they aren't necessarily face-to-face. This can also happen through a group chat using the Internet or text messaging. Another form of communication is Intrapersonal. This is done when an individual communicates with themselves usually in their mind. The mass-media industry "employs professionals to conceive, produce, promote, and deliver communication products that are specifically designed to meet the goal of attracting large audiences" . These products "may be sold as objects (such as books or digital videodiscs [DVDs]), exhibited for the price of a ticket or subscription (such as movies shown in cinemas or on premium or pay-for-view cable TV channels), or offered at no cash cost to consumers so as to create an audience for paid advertising (such as commercial television or radio broadcasts)" . "Some of the mass media use combinations of these funding sources; for example, most newspapers and magazines are sold directly to the reader but depend on selling advertisements for their profitability".

Functions of Mass Media

There are four major functions of mass media. The first is for surveillance. This is to provide information about issues, events and developments in society. The second is correlation. Media must interpret events and issues and ascribe meaning so that individuals understand their roles in society. A term that best fits with correlation is agenda setting, which means the media doesn't tell you what to think, but what to think about. Media tells you what is and isn't important and to what degree, but that will be covered in a later chapter. Next is cultural transmission. This is where the media aids the transference of dominant cultures and subcultures from one generation to the next or to immigrants. The last function of mass media is to simply entertain (Pavlik & McIntosh, 2004). According to Pavlik & McIntosh, 2004, there is a standard, overarching model for mass communication that has been used since the invention of the first printing press. The model has four main points. The first is "communication flow is largely one-way, from sender or source to receiver or audience" . The second, "communication is from one or a few to many". Third, "communication is anonymous (sources generally do not know their audiences and audience do not know the sources, except at a general level)" Fourth, "audiences are largely seen as passive recipients of the messages distributed by the media, with little opportunity for feedback and practically no opportunity for immediate feedback or interaction with one another" This model refers to movies/films, books, newspapers, television, radio, or any other form of mass media. It states that mass communication isn't interactive, audiences and senders are unknown to one another and it can only flow one way.

Media Convergence

Media convergence is known "broadly as the coming together of computing, telecommunications, and media in a digital environment" (Pavlik & McIntosh, 2004,). There are three major categories for media convergence. These categories are technological convergence, economic convergence and cultural convergence. The first, technological convergence has to do with traditional media converging into a digital platform. This is referring to traditional media such as print, audio and video converging with digital media. An example of this would be a journalist having to report highlights of a news story on Twitter or conducting a podcast. Journalists sometimes have to be interactive, especially on social media, and not just robots giving information. Technological convergences changes the experience consumers have with traditional media. . Economic Convergence is the merging of Internet, or telecommunication companies, with more traditional media companies. . According to Pavilk & McIntosh, 2004, traditional media companies "have grown fewer and much larger in the past 50 years through mergers and acquisitions" . The last is cultural convergence. This pertains to the beliefs, values and practices shared by a group of people. It is the "process of globalization of media content"

.

Effects of Mass Media

Media today is forever changing. The fact that technology evolves and changes "drives the development of media" (Grolier Multimedia Encyclopedia, 2013). Because we as a society are always using mass media there are consequences and effects that have been laid on the forefront of mass media. Certain scholars, scientist and researchers "believe that the mass media shape the way people view the world, especially when people have little direct experience; others point to the media as providing role models—positive and negative—imitated by members of the audience" . The portrayal of violence in the media seems to be the most talked about issue, but other "behavioral areas are of concern". These arguments tend to be based on "the supposition that the experience of the content presented by contemporary mass media differs in some qualitative way from other material that people have been exposed to since the beginning of social communication" . Attempts to "hold mass-media corporations legally responsible for the criminal acts of the consumers of their products have failed, and a general consensus has been reached that people will have to continue to be responsible for their own behaviors in the age of mass media" .Social Media are Internet sites where people interact freely, sharing and discussing information about each other and their lives, using a multimedia mix of personal words, pictures, videos and audio.

Internet

The Internet is a worldwide system of interconnected computer networks. The computers and computer networks exchange information using TCP/IP (Transmission Control Protocol/Internet Protocol) to communicate with each other. The computers are connected via the telecommunications networks, and the Internet can be used for e-mailing, transferring files and accessing information on the World Wide Web.

The World Wide Web is a system of Internet servers that use HTTP (Hypertext Transfer Protocol) to transfer documents formatted in HTML (Hypertext Mark-up

Language). These are viewed by using software for web browsers such as Netscape and Internet Explorer. Hypertext enables a document to be connected to other documents on the web through hyperlinks. It is possible to move from one document to another by using hyperlinked text found within web pages

Nowadays, there are several ways that enable us to access the Internet. Technology is keep improving, method to access the Internet also increase. People can now access Internet services by using their cell phone, laptop and various gadgets. The numbers of Internet service providers are also keep increasing. For example in Malaysia, there are many Internet service providers such as TM Net, Maxis , Digi, Celcom, Umobile, etc.

Communication is becoming much easier than before due to the appearance of Internet. One of the conveniences is that messages, in the forms of email, can be sent at any corner of the world within fractions of seconds. Besides that, email also facilitated mass communication which means that one sender reaches many receivers. Some of the services made available due to Internet include video conferencing, live telecast, music, news, e-commerce, etc.

Internet usage and benefit

It is globalization and modernization nowadays, Internet become more and more useful and come into everyday life. So we need to understand its social impact and the behaviors leading to this impact. Let us study why people using Internet for certain reasons and some benefits from it. From the early days of computers to now, communication between people to people has been the technology's most frequent used. People using the Internet to sent or received email. Using email leads people to spend more time online, encourages their use of the Internet for information, entertainment. All this can save time and money because it is consider efficiency enough and always is cheaper. As new Internet communication services arise such as those instant messaging, chat rooms, online games, auctions (eBay), and my groups, they become instantly popular.

Information searching is the second basic Internet function. Many use the Internet to search and download some of the free, useful computer software that provided by the developers on computers worldwide. The only major problem would be finding what you need among the storehouses of data found in databases and libraries. It is therefore necessary to explain the two major methods of accessing computers and locating files without the information retrieval function would not be possible. There are also educational resources on the Internet. They are in various forms such as journals and databases on different types of knowledge. For example, people can access online journals, or learning languages. There are also special homepages on special topics or subjects of interest. These sites are very helpful to those who are doing academic research or even teachers. This will go a long way to improve their knowledge to make them more competitive and knowledgeable. There are now even virtual libraries and full degree programs, all available online.

In fact, it is undeniable a trend of commerce on the Internet. The communication facilities have now rapidly become integrated as core business tools such as Internet market, banking, advertisement and so on. Thus most of the business functions are communicative in nature. Users or consumer need not to waste their time on queue up waiting their transaction and service. Internet makes communication with customers and other business partner even to some respondent if related to some online survey.

To conclude, using the Internet in the right way, give lots of benefits.

Internet Application

Network applications are among the most important parts in computer network – if we couldn't get any useful applications, there would be no use designing networking protocols to support them. Over half a century ago, a variety of intelligent network applications were created. These applications included the classic text-based applications that become popular in the 1970s and later developed into e-mail, remote access to computers, file transfers, newsgroup and text chat in 1980s. As time went by they introduced more killer applications like the World Wide Web, encompassing Web surfing, search and electronic commerce in middle 1990s. Applications like instant messaging with buddy list and P2P file sharing were introduced at the end of millennium.

Nowadays, instead of the already applications was updated, they also include successful audio and video applications including Internet telephony, video sharing and streaming, social networking applications, Internet radio and IP television (IPTV). In addition, the increased penetration of residential broadband access and ubiquity increased access wireless applications set the stage for an exciting future. At the core of the network applications development writing programs that take place on different end systems communicated with each other through the network.

For example, the Web application, there are two different programs that communicate with each other: the browser program running on the user's host desktop, laptop. PDA, cell phone and so on; and the Web server program running in the Web server host. As another example, in a P2P file sharing systems have a program in each host community to participate in file sharing. In this case, the programs on the various hosts may be similar or identical. This basic design – namely, confining application software to the end.

Television

Television's substantial impact on all growing children began in the 1950s with the proliferation of TV sets. Three generations of children have been raised with TV, and very different role models, interaction modes, and experiences are now visited on American youth. Today, more than 99% of American households contain at least one television set, and children start the viewing process early even before they reach 2 years of age. Conservative estimates are that preschool children watch nearly 3.5 hours of TV per day (Gentile & Walsh, 2002), and this average continues through age 18 (Singer & Singer, 2001). In the 21st century, however, television viewing is becoming somewhat diminished because of increased use of computer games and the Internet, and also because children now spend more time in child-care, school, and after-school-care programs.

Television influences children in direct proportion to both time spent viewing and the overall effect of what is viewed (American Academy of Pediatrics, 1990). Certainly, eating habits, family interactions, and use of leisure time are considerably influenced by television (Hewlett & West, 2005; Horgen, 2005;

Winn, 2002). Commercials take up 12 to 14 minutes of every hour of television, and in that time, advertisers try to influence viewers with all types of consumerism. Schools and parents are far behind advertisers in finding the most effective ways of using media.

Children are especially susceptible to electronic media, and televised advertising has a huge effect. Heavy viewers are drawn to the advertised products, including unhealthy food products, and they tend to eat more snack foods and be overweight. Social interactions are also affected: Heavy viewers hold more traditional sex-role attitudes, behave more aggressively, are less socially competent, and perform more poorly in school compared to light or non viewers. (Arendell, 1997; Desmond, 2001).

Not all TV advertising is negative, of course. There have been efforts through TV to modify behaviors such as smoking, drunken driving, and poor nutritional habits (Van Evra, 2004). How children are affected by both positive and negative advertisements also depends on such factors as parent–child interactions, how children are disciplined, and even to some degree on social–economic factors (Strasburger & Wilson, 2002).

Advertising is not the only way in which television influences viewers. Two additional, concerns about the effects of television are the amount of violence, in both commercials and programs, and the amount of time children's television watching takes away from more creative and intellectual pursuits.

Research on the impact of television viewing on academic achievement indicates that such influence is complex in nature. Television viewing takes time away from important social interactions, such as conversation, storytelling, imaginative play, and for primary-school children, the leisure reading that promotes literacy. We must remember, however, that the amount of viewing, the kind of programs watched, IQ, and socioeconomic status are all factors that affect children's attitude and achievement (Gunter, Harrison, & Wykes, 2003; Winn, 2002).

The average child watches nearly 14 h of television each week. By his/her high school graduation, the average teen will have spent more time watching television than in the classroom. Studies show time spent watching television varies between different age groups and cultures. This is especially relevant when studying the effects of excessive television exposure on disadvantaged populations.

The amount of time that younger children currently spend watching television has not decreased significantly. A substantial number of children begin watching television at an earlier age and in greater amounts than what experts recommend. Evidence suggests that television's influence on children and adolescents is related to how much time they spend watching television. As a result, with prolonged viewing, the world shown on television becomes the real world.

Television viewing frequently limits children's time for vital activities such as playing, reading, learning to talk, spending time with peers and family, storytelling, participating in regular exercise, and developing other necessary physical, mental and social skills. In addition to the amount of time spent in front of the television, other factors that influence the medium's effect on children include the child's developmental level, individual susceptibility and whether children watch television alone or with their parents.

Learning

Television can be a powerful teacher. Watching *Sesame Street* is an example of how toddlers can learn valuable lessons about racial harmony, cooperation, kindness, simple arithmetic and the alphabet through an educational television format. Some public television programs stimulate visits to the zoo, libraries, bookstores, museums and other active recreational settings, and educational videos can certainly serve as powerful pro social teaching devices. The educational value of *Sesame Street*, has been shown to improve the reading and learning skills of its viewers. In some disadvantaged settings, healthy television habits may actually be a beneficial teaching tool.

Still, watching television takes time away from reading and schoolwork. More recent and well-controlled studies show that even 1 h to 2 h of daily unsupervised television viewing by school-aged children has a significant deleterious effect on academic performance, especially reading.

Violence

The amount of violence on television is on the rise. The average child sees 12,000 violent acts on television annually, including many depictions of murder and rape. More than 1000 studies confirm that exposure to heavy doses of television violence increases aggressive behaviour, particularly in boys. Studies link television or newspaper publicity of suicides to an increased suicide risk.

The following groups of children may be more vulnerable to violence on television:

- children from minority and immigrant groups;
- emotionally disturbed children;
- children with learning disabilities;
- children who are abused by their parents; and
- children in families in distress.

Nutrition

Because television takes time away from play and exercise activities, children who watch a lot of television are less physically fit and more likely to eat high fat and high energy snack foods. Television viewing makes a substantial contribution to obesity because prime time commercials promote unhealthy dietary practices. The fat content of advertised products exceeds the current average Canadian diet and nutritional recommendations, and most food advertising is for high calorie foods such as fast foods, candy and presweetened cereals. Commercials for healthy food make up only 4% of the food advertisements shown during children's viewing time. The number of hours of television viewing also corresponds with an increased relative risk of higher cholesterol levels in children. Television can also contribute to eating disorders in teenage girls, who may emulate the thin role models seen on television. Eating meals while watching television should be discouraged because it may lead to less meaningful communication and, arguably, poorer eating habits.

Cognitive development ---

Cognitive development is field of study in neuroscience and psychology focusing on a child's development in terms of information processing, conceptual resources, perceptual skill, language learning, and other aspects of brain development and cognitive psychology compared to an adult's point of view. In other words, cognitive development is the emergence of the ability to think and understand. A large portion of research has gone into understanding how a child imagines the world. Jean Piaget was a major force in the establishment of this field, forming his "theory of cognitive development". Piaget proposed four stages of cognitive development.

Historical Origins: Piaget's theory of cognitive development

Jean Piaget (1896-1980) believed that people move through stages of development that allow them to think in new, more complex ways.

Sensor motor stage

The first stage in Piaget's Stages of Cognitive Development is the sensor motor stage. This stage lasts from birth to two years old. During this stage, behaviors lack a sense of thought and logic. Behaviors gradually move from acting upon inherited reflexes to interacting with the environment with a goal in mind and being able to represent the external world at the end.

The sensori motor stage has been broken down into six sub stages that explain the gradual development of infants at this age.

Birth to one month

Each child is born with inherited reflexes that they use to gain knowledge and understanding about their environment. *Examples of these reflexes include grasping and sucking*

1–4 months

Children repeat behaviors that happen unexpectedly because of their reflexes.

For example, a child's finger comes in contact with the mouth and the child starts sucking on it. If the sensation is pleasurable to the child, then the child will attempt to recreate the behavior. Infants use their initial reflexes (grasping and sucking) to explore their environment and create schemes. Schemes are groups of similar actions or thoughts that are used repeatedly in response to the environment. Once a child begins to create schemes they use accommodation and assimilation to become progressively adapted to the world **Assimilation** is when a child responds to a new event in a way that is consistent with an existing schema. *For example, an infant may assimilate a new teddy bear into their putting things in their mouth scheme and use their reflexes to make the teddy bear go into their mouth.* **Accommodation** is when a child either modifies an existing scheme or forms an entirely new schema to deal with a new object or event. *For example, an infant may have to open his or her mouth wider than usual to accommodate the teddy bear's paw.*

5–8 months

Child has an experience with an external stimulus that they find pleasurable, so they try to recreate that experience. *For example, a child accidentally hits the mobile above the crib and likes to watch it spin. When it stops the child begins to grab at the object to make it spin again.*In this stage habits are formed from general schemes that the infant has created but there is not yet, from the child's point of view, any differentiation between means and ends. Children cannot also focus on multiple tasks at once, and only focus on the task at hand. The child may create a habit of spinning the mobile in its crib, but they are still trying to find out methods to reach the mobile in order to get it to spin in the way that they find pleasurable. Once there is another distraction (say the parent walks in the room) the baby will no longer focus on the mobile. Toys should be given to infants that respond to a child's actions to help foster their investigative instincts. *For example, a toy plays a song when you push one button, and then a picture pops up if you push another button.*

8–12 months

Behaviors will be displayed for a reason rather than by chance. They begin to understand that one action can cause a reaction. They also begin to understand **object permanence**, which is the realization that objects continue to exist when removed form view. *For example: The baby wants a rattle but the blanket is in the way. The baby moves the blanket to get the rattle.* Now that the infant can understand that the object still exists, they can differentiate between the object, and the experience of the object. According to psychologist David Elkind, "An internal representation of the absent object is the earliest manifestation of the symbolic function which develops gradually during the second year of life whose activities dominate the next stage of mental growth."

12–18 months

Actions occur deliberately with some variation. *For example a baby drums on a pot with a wooden spoon, then drums on the floor, then on the table.*

18 - 24 months

Children begin to build mental symbols and start to participate in pretend play. *For example, a child is mixing ingredients together but doesn't have a spoon so they pretend to use one or use another object the replace the spoon* **Symbolic thought** is a representation of objects and events as mental entities or symbols which helps foster cognitive development and the formation of imagination. According to Piaget, the infant begins to act upon intelligence rather than habit at this point. The end product is established after the infant has pursued for the appropriate means. The means are formed from the schemes that are known by the child. The child is starting to learn how to use what it has learned in the first two years to develop and further explore their environment.

These six sub-stages represent the approximate growth a child undergoes during Piaget's sensori motor stage from birth to age 2. Once the child gains the ability to mentally represent reality, the child begins the transition to the preoperational stage of development.

Preoperational stage

Lasts from 2 years of age until 6 or 7. It can be characterized in two somewhat different ways. In his early work, before he had developed his structuralist theory of cognition, Piaget described the child's thought during this period as being governed by principles such as egocentrism, animism and other similar constructs. Egocentrism is when a child can only see a certain situation his or her own way. One cannot comprehend that other people have other views and perceptions of scenarios. Animism is when an individual gives a lifeless object human like qualities. An individual usually believes that this object has human emotions, thoughts and intentions. Once he had proposed his structuralist theory, Piaget characterized the preoperational child as lacking the cognitive structures possessed by the concrete operational child. The absence of these structures explains, in part, the behaviors Piaget had previously described as egocentric and animistic, for example an inability to comprehend that another individual may have different emotional responses to similar experiences. During this stage children also become increasingly adept at using symbols as evidenced by the increase in playing and pretending.

Concrete operational stage

Lasts from 6 or 7 years until about 12 or 13. During this stage the child's cognitive structures can be characterized by group therapy. Piaget argues that the same general principles can be discerned in a wide range of behaviors. One of the best-known achievements of this stage is that of conservation. In a typical conservation experiment a child is asked to judge whether or not two quantities are the same – such as two equal quantities of liquid in a short and tall glass. A preoperational child will typically judge the taller, thinner glass to contain more, while a concrete operational child will judge the amounts still to be the same. The ability to reason in this way reflects the development of a principle of conservation.

Emotional development-

Along with physical and cognitive development, every child progresses through phases of emotional development. Arguably, all children differ in their individual development. Studies have shown that parents admit to having little information on emotional development, even though they also admit that their actions have great influence on their children's emotional development.

Emotions are not as easy to study or recognize as cognition, and for many decades the study of emotional development lagged behind study in other areas of child development. However, by the early twenty-first century researchers had developed several theories on emotional development.

Emotional development definition

Emotional development is the emergence of a child's experience, expression, understanding, and regulation of emotions from birth through late adolescence. It also comprises how growth and changes in these processes concerning emotions occur. Emotional development does not occur in isolation; neural, cognitive, and behavioral development interact with emotional development and social and cultural influences, and context also play a role. Various emotional development theories are proposed, but there is general agreement on age-related milestones in emotional development.

Social and emotional development are strongly linked and sometimes studied or reported in tandem. Parents and other caregivers play an important role in emotional development, but as a child's world expands, other people in the social context also play a part in emotional development.

Debate continues as to exactly when emotions appear in infants. For example, smiles occur early, but the earliest ones are more likely reflexive than social. A smile may express emotion as early as 6 weeks of age but it is not until about age 6 months that a smile can be considered more emotional and social in nature. Crying is a powerful emotion for infants and may be used as a communication tool. Distress, pleasure, anger, fear, and interest are among the earliest emotions that infants express. Laughter begins at about 3 to 4 months of age. Eliciting laughter in babies at this age often involves an action that deviates from the norm, such as peek-a-boo games provoke. Development of negative emotions probably follows soon after, with anger still winning over sadness to express negative feelings. Fear begins to emerge, and infants often follow the emotions of their caregivers and form strong attachment to them.

By toddlerhood and early childhood, children begin to develop more of a sense of self. Emotions such as pride, shame, and self-recognition begin to emerge. These developments are facilitated partly by the rapid maturation of a toddler's frontal lobes and limbic circuit in the brain. These emotional developments lead to the strong sense of independence and defiance that often characterize the toddler years. Of course, toddlers also are becoming more independent physically, having developed skills such as walking. They may begin to play independently too. The self-recognition brings new levels of emotional development. For example, toddlers will begin to respond to negative signals from caregivers and others. It is at the toddler stage, or at least by age 2, that children also begin showing empathy, which is a complex emotional response to a situation. Feeling empathy requires that a child not only read emotional clues from others but understand the distinction between self and others. Actually putting one's self in the other's position also is required for empathy.

Emotional expression is still largely nonverbal, although some emotional language may develop by age 20 months. For the most part, facial expressions, crying or other vocal expressions, and gestures still express many of toddlers' emotions. In early childhood, verbal skills develop and with them, verbal reasoning. Children also are able to talk about their feelings as they learn how to express themselves verbally. As young children enter preschool, they may be able to label their emotions and learn about them by understanding family discussions and actions concerning emotions. For example, a child may be able to say, "I am mad," or "I am sad," instead of simply expressing the emotion through actions such as crying, stomping, or yelling. This is not to say that tantrums do not occur; between toddlerhood and school age, children still express anger in the form of tantrums. Because emotions have become important to young children, they talk about them often in conversation.

Preschoolers begin to understand the rules of family, school, and society concerning how they express some of their emotions. They also can recognize nonverbal cues of emotion from one another. Preschoolers begin to distinguish between negative emotions such as sadness, anger, and fear. Although these young children have empathy, their knowledge of others' feelings generally is limited to people and situations with which they are familiar. Development of this emotional capacity also depends on positive, culturally acceptable emotional exchanges with peers. Negative emotional influences of family life that are common and harsh, particularly in the child's discipline model, can lead to problems with emotional development and even psychopathology

Basic emotions

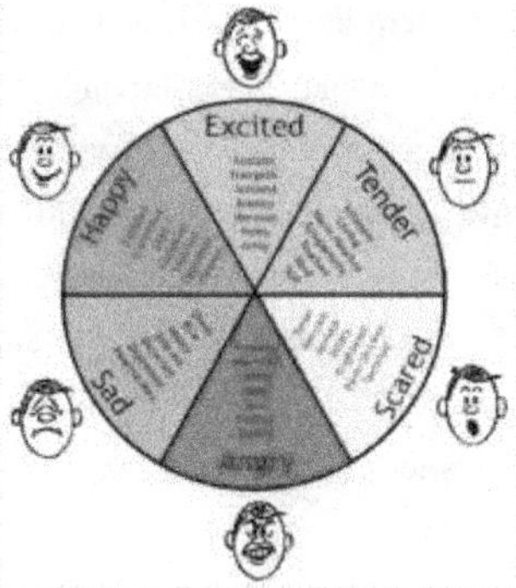

Entering school

As children enter school, they gain a greater sense of self and an understanding of how specific situations can lead them to experience emotions. Children may experience shame, even in reaction to emotions expressed. They also can begin to understand how an event can lead to mixed emotions. Research has shown that by about age 6, children may appreciate that people can experience one emotion, then a completely different emotion immediately after the first. The understanding of simultaneous and even conflicting emotions soon follows.

As children move into later childhood, they learn the "rules" of displaying emotion, which is a form of social and emotional development. For example, if children have been taught to do so, they may, out of politeness or respect, be able to avoid showing disappointment in a gift or the failure of an adult to fulfill a promise. As they understand the emotional states of those around them, children realize that these states are not as simple as they might have once imagined.

School-aged children begin developing emotional coping skills, even if those skills are at very basic levels. For example, children may rationalize situations and behaviors or reconstruct scenarios to make them seem less upsetting emotionally. The ability to suppress negative emotions is a factor of normal development, as well as other influences, such as gender, the specific situation, cultural influences, and the person likely to receive the expressed emotion.

In adolescence emotions still are developing. In face, the adolescent years often are considered an emotional period of development. Although adolescents begin to develop independence from their parents and begin to display social signs of independence by gaining employment, driving, and other activities, their emotional autonomy is represented by conflict and often negative emotions. One reason for the negative emotions may be cognitive development of abstract thinking abilities. Because adolescents can imagine all sorts of complex and theoretical scenarios for romance or in response to other relationships, they may suffer resulting emotional distress. In turn, social problems become more complex, and adolescents look to their peers to help provide a basis for how to manage the emotions they feel.

Family issues and struggles over becoming independent, with curfews, academic pressure, and romantic and other peer interactions, all place a great deal of pressure on adolescent emotions. Strong self-perceptions from earlier childhood may give way to self-doubt or feelings of worthlessness. As adolescents realize that their emotions are separate from their parents' emotions, a process called "emotional autonomy" begins. Adolescents may feel pulled between the close emotional ties they have with their parents and a need to develop independent emotional responses. If depression is going to occur, it generally begins during adolescence and is more common in girls than in boys.

Emotional regulation

A major part of emotional development in children and adolescents is how children recognize, label, and control the expression of their emotions in ways that generally are consistent with cultural expectations. This is called emotional regulation. In short, development of an emotion almost is dependent on regulation. The exact definition and models of emotional regulation have been debated. But what is apparent in the study of child and adolescent development and the development of positive instructional strategies is the complex interaction of emotional regulation and development of emotions.

Self-regulation of emotions includes recognition and delineation of emotions. Once a child can articulate an emotion, the articulation already has a somewhat regulatory effect. Children may be able to use various techniques to self-regulate as they develop and mature. Children begin learning at a young age to control certain negative emotions when in the presence of adults, but not to control them as much around peers. By about age 4, children begin to learn how to alter how they express emotions to suit what they feel others expect them to express. The ability to do so is what psychologists call *emotional display rules*.

By about age 7 to 11 years, children are better able to regulate their emotions and to use a variety of self-regulation skills. They have likely developed expectations concerning the outcome that expressing a particular emotion to others might produce and have developed a menu of behavioral skills to control how they express their emotions. By adolescence, they adapt these skills to specific social relationships. For example, older children may express negative emotions more often to their mothers than to their fathers because they assume their fathers will react negatively to displays of emotion. Adolescents also have heightened sensitivity to how others evaluate them. Their self-consciousness and the culture-specific nature of guidelines concerning the appropriateness of emotional expression make this a particularly difficult time to learn when and how to express or regulate many emotions.

Several emotional development models and perspectives present views on emotional regulation. The functionalist perspective emphasizes that emotions serve a function of focusing action to achieve personal goals. Self-regulation is critical to emotional development because it marks a progressive ability to regulate emotions according to demands of the physical and social worlds. Actions match the demands of the situation and each family of emotions provides a range of behavior-regulatory, social-regulatory, and internal-regulatory functions for an individual.

The perspective of emotions as discrete states is based on understanding emotions as patterns of configurations in the brain, as demonstrated in cognitive neuro-scientific studies. Neurochemical processes result in subjective feeling states, with accompanying automatic changes in bodily function and behavior. These give rise to basic emotions. Specific sections of the brain are associated with particular emotions. For example, the right prefrontal cortex is associated with negative affect and withdrawal. Theorists propose a maturational timetable for emergence of these basic emotions, beginning in infancy. Emotional development and regulation are dependent on cognition for the most part; cognitive development leads to new abilities to understand and self-regulate basic emotions.

Process viewpoints, also known as systems perspectives, do not disclaim the functional utility of emotions or their grounding in discrete feeling states. But the perspectives focus on how emotions emerge from one's tendency to self-organize various interacting components. These components include felt experiences, cognitive appraisals, motivations, functions, and control elements. This perspective leaves emotional regulation dynamic and open to transformation, as emotions are complex and specific to situations. They also help form the basis of one's self and personality. Like functional and discrete state perspectives, systems theories maintain that emotions can serve adaptive functions for a child, especially in social situations.

Emotion s at school

The interplay of emotional development, social development, and academic performance is complex. C. Cybele Raver's 2002 research has established a strong link between social/emotional development and behavior and school success, particularly in the first few years of schooling. If a child's academic tasks are interrupted by problems with peers, following directions, or controlling negative emotions, the child will have trouble learning to read or staying on task in other educational activities. Research also has linked antisocial behavior with decreased academic performance.

Emotional understanding can positively relate to adaptive social behavior, yet it can negatively relate to internalizing behavior. This may lead to feelings of anxiety, depression, and loneliness. Knowledge of emotion can affect verbal ability, and in turn, academic competence. Verbal and prosocial skills are critical to academic achievement. For example, a child must be able to communicate with his or her teacher, which includes reading emotional cues. Children who do not learn to regulate emotions and who display disruptive behavior in school spend less time on tasks and receive less instruction and less positive feedback.

How To Support The Emotional Development of Child

Children need a lot of care from their parents. They require both financial and moral support during their entire development. Even though some parents may consider that providing their children with financial support is the most important aspect out of these two, they could not be more wrong. Moral and emotional support are crucial for a normal social and emotional development of a child.

As a child grows and develops, his ability to deal with emotional issues also increases. Depending on how well you help your child learn how to deal with intensive emotional charged events, he will cope with stress successfully or deeply suffer from all changes that occur in his lifetime.

Source

Below you can find some tips on how to support the emotional development of your child. Keep them in mind and you can be absolutely sure that your kid will enjoy a normal emotional development.

- One of the main aspects that should be mentioned here is that you should start early to help your child develop a healthy emotional response system. Encourage your child all the time, no matter if the steps made are small. One of the most common mistakes that parents make is not allowing their children to be independent. You have to encourage all steps that your baby makes to independence. For instance, if your kid wants to prepare his own meals, you should let him, even though he may be too young for that.
- Create a nurturing atmosphere in your home. Affection and understanding is all you need to achieve this purpose. Your child has to know that he has all the support he may need from you. Your son or daughter has to be sure that he or she can come to you with anything.
- Avoid comparing your child with other children. Children are different and they all have their own rate of development. Raising a child is one of the hardest jobs in the world. There is no race. All children must follow their own rhythm on becoming emotionally secure adults.
- Use positive examples in the relationship with your child. Children usually see their parents as a source of inspiration. If you deal great with stress and you constantly maintain a positive attitude, your child will easily learn that from your behavior.

Source

Encourage your children to be open to you. Your kids should be encouraged to voice their ideas and easily solve stressful situations. Teach them how important it is to respect other children and adults. Encourage your kids to make a lot of friends, as they have an important contribution to social and emotional development, too. Being a great parent and sustaining the social development of your kids is not that hard. You only have to know some simple ways in which you can achieve this purpose.

Social development-

Social development involves learning the values, knowledge and skills that enable children to relate to others effectively and to contribute in positive ways to family, school and the community. This kind of learning is passed on to children directly by those who care for and teach them, as well as indirectly through social relationships within the family or with friends, and through children's participation in the culture around them. Through their relationships with others and their growing awareness of social values and expectations, children build a sense of who they are and of the social roles available to them. As children develop socially, they both respond to the influences around them and play an active part in shaping their relationships.

Influences on children's social development

While parents and careers are clearly the first and most important influencers on children's social development, there are many other influential aspects of the social environment.

The people and settings that are most closely involved with the child – family, school and peers – are shown at the centre of the diagram. Through their daily contact with parents, careers, family members, school staff, as well as with their peers, children learn about the social world and about the rules, practices and values that support it. By actively participating in these relationships, children also affect the ways that adults and their peers relate to them.

In addition, children's development is influenced by wider networks of social support (represented in the diagram's central circles), including extended family, friends and any community, cultural or religious groups a child may be part of. These networks provide opportunities for children to develop their social awareness and skills as they relate with different people and experience a range of roles and expectations.

As shown in the outer circle in the diagram, children's lives are also shaped by the broader social circumstances that impact on their families and communities, such as access to social and health services, parents' employment and income, or their ability to balance work and family time. In particular, children's sense of social connection is often influenced by community attitudes and by cultural values, including those they encounter in the media.

Through their relationships and connections with others, children build a sense of who they are and where they fit in the social world. Coming to an understanding about self and others is therefore a central goal of children's social development.

Developmental trends in children's self-concept

The ideas, beliefs and knowledge that children have about who they are, what they can do and where they fit in society help to shape their understanding of themselves. Children base their self-concepts on feedback they receive from others as well as their own judgments. The kinds of things that primary school children take into account in developing their self-concepts include how well they are able to succeed with schoolwork and other activities, how they look, and how they get on with family and peers. Developmental patterns in the ways children typically describe themselves are related to their developing capacities for thinking and for understanding and managing their emotions and behaviour. As shown in the following table, preschool children often have very high opinions of their abilities. During primary school, children become much more aware of how their abilities and achievements compare with those of others.

Typical developmental changes in children's self-concepts		
Developmental stage	What children might say about themselves	What it shows
Preschool	"I am four years old. I live with my Mum and Dad and my little sister. I love to play football. I can kick the ball really far. Watch me!"	Describes physical appearance, family context and favourite activity. Has high opinion of own abilities and wants to show you.
Primary school	"I am pretty good at maths because I get good marks. But I'm not so good at English, not like Sophie. Kids like to play with me because I'm happy most of the time and I'm kind."	Compares self with others. Determines own ability level by ranking performance against that of peers. Able to make a (more) realistic assessment of own abilities.
Secondary school	"I'm pretty talkative and funny with my friends. I'm an extrovert. At home I can be pretty moody. I get annoyed with my parents because they always seem to be on my back. But, I guess, where would I be without them?"	Able to reflect on and evaluate own qualities. Understands and accepts that personal characteristics can be changeable and inconsistent. Is able to integrate them into a coherent sense of

Typical developmental changes in children's self-concepts		
Developmental stage	What children might say about themselves	What it shows
		self.

It is very important for children's strengths and efforts to be recognised in order to support the development of a positive self-concept and to motivate children to be positively engaged in learning and in their relationships. Poor self-concept can be a significant contributing factor to children's emotional and behavioural difficulties.

Culture and self-concept

Having a strong cultural identity enhances children's self-concept and promotes a sense of connectedness and belonging. Children's cultural identity is nurtured when they learn about their own cultural traditions and when those around them show respect for their cultural values. Teaching children to respect and appreciate variations and differences between cultures is therefore very important for all children's social development.

Children from minority cultural groups can encounter differences between the rules and expectations required at school and those they are used to at home. When the differences are not acknowledged, or when the cultural traditions children identify with are ignored or minimised, it can negatively affect children's cultural identity development and sense of belonging.

Children from minority cultures may be subjected to stereotyping and discrimination on the basis of their ethnicity, religion, gender, appearance, social class or sexuality. Discrimination and bullying can have serious effects on children's mental health and wellbeing as well as their social development. By contrast, overcoming discrimination has been found to have positive effects on self-concept. It is very important for parents, careers and school staff to encourage and support children to take positive action against discrimination and bullying by speaking up and reporting incidents.

Learning social values

Children's ability to understand others and take their needs and views into account develops over time. Young children are naturally self-focussed. They often play beside, rather than with, other children and tend to think that everyone sees things the same way that they do. In early primary school children learn that others may see things differently from them. Then, as their thinking skills develop, children are more able to understand another person's point of view and, finally, to appreciate multiple ways of looking at the same event or situation.

Teaching children how to put themselves in someone else's shoes helps them to relate better to others and manage conflict more effectively. It promotes caring, respect and fairness. Research shows that children who have learned to value others are more likely to include and appreciate children who are different from them or who are viewed negatively by others.

Research into moral development has highlighted how social behaviour reflects the attitudes people hold about social conventions and about themselves. Learning to take account of others' feelings, perspectives and expectations contributes to children's understanding of social values, and to the values and ethics they choose for themselves. Using an example where children have broken the window of a neighbour's car playing a game, the following table shows how children use different moral reasoning to decide what to do and say.

Children learn to make ethical judgments through having practice in putting themselves in others' shoes and through being encouraged to reflect on issues that involve social and moral values. Families and schools can work together to help children understand and learn to act on values like respect, responsibility, caring for others, honesty, cooperation and acceptance of people's differences.

Key points for supporting children's social development

Children's earliest and most extensive learning about social relationships occurs in the family. Parents and careers can support positive social development when they model respect and consideration and encourage children to be similarly respectful in all their relationships.

Provide care and support by tuning into children's needs. Show you are willing to listen and take children's feelings into consideration.

Help children to develop social skills by providing coaching and teaching them to think through and solve the day-to-day social difficulties they encounter. Supervise and support children's social activities without taking over.

Ask questions that encourage children to put themselves in someone else's shoes. Questions like "How would you feel if …?" help children learn skills for perspective-taking. Asking questions in a supportive way helps children to think through situations and encourages them to take others' feelings and perspectives into account.

Discuss moral issues with children and encourage them to state their opinions and reasons.

CHAPTER- 2

REVIEW OF LITERATURE

Review of related literature implies, locating, studying and evaluating ports of relevant researches, published articles, related portions of encyclopedia and research abstracts. For any worthwhile study in field of knowledge the research worker needs an adequate familiarity with the work that has already been done in the area of his chosen field.

Review of related literature is an important research effort as it provides comprehensive understanding of what is already known about the topic. The main functions of citing review of literature is to provide a basis for developing a frame work. Familiarity with research work of others provides up-to-date knowledge of the latest developments, findings, recommendations, tools and loop holes of researches. It helps to avoid duplication of what has already been done, and provides useful directions and helpful suggestions for research work. Thus an attempt has been made in this chapter to review the studies related to this investigation.

The mass media, particularly television, influence childhood development by providing opportunities for modeling and information-seeking outside family and school. Americans in all age groups tend to spend more time watching television than any activity other than sleeping. The average American child has been estimated to watch over 20,000 television commercials per year in addition to the commercial programming interspersed between them. In 2000, children two to five years old watched 40 hours of television per week and children six to eleven years old watched 50-60 hours per week. Thus the messages that television conveys not only represents the culture in which they appear but are also a large part of it.

One of the notable changes in our social environment in the 21st century has been the saturation of our culture and daily lives by the mass media. Unfortunately, the consequences of one particular common element of the electronic mass media have a particularly detrimental effect on children's well being. It is now not just kids in bad neighborhoods or with "bad" friends who are likely to be exposed to bad things when they go out on the street. A "virtual" bad street is easily available to most youth now in their very homes.

Radio, television (TV), movies, video games, cell phones, and computer networks have assumed central roles in our children's daily lives. The media has demonstrated potentially profound effects, both positive and negative, on children's cognitive, social, and behavioral development. Considering the increasing exposure of children to newer forms of media, we have to review the current literature on the effects of media on child health both in the Western countries and India. It is widely accepted that media has profound influence on child health, including violence, obesity, tobacco and alcohol use, and risky sexual behaviors. Simultaneously, media may have some positive effects on child health. We need to find ways to optimize the role of media in our society, taking advantage of their positive attributes and minimizing their negative
ones. We need to understand better how to reverse the negative impact of media and make it more positive.

Stereotypical behavior by females and males characterizes both children's and adult's programming, as well as commercials. For example, a study of Saturday morning children's programs found that 68% of the major characters were male and that male characters engaged in more activity than female characters. Boys thereby had the greater opportunity to imitate same-sex models than girls. Also, the sexes tended to appear in different roles. Females were more often presented in relationships with others such as family or friends, while males were more often portrayed in roles independent of others or at work (Giddens A. (2006)). I
n commercials, males were presented as more knowledgeable and females as more bewildered. Here we see the familiar pattern of males seeming more important, deserving of more attention, and more in command of themselves and the situation. Not surprisingly, both children and adults who watch more television tend to be more aware of gender stereotypes, see themselves in more

stereotypical terms and hold more traditional attitudes toward men's and women's roles. Modern art changes and deforms the children's psychic setup, exerts influence upon their imagination, giving new guidelines and models of behavior. Into children's consciousness false and dangerous values burst from the virtual world outside, values like: the cult of power, aggression, rude and vulgar behavior; all of these lead to hyper excitability of children. Often in cartoons the accent is put on aggression (Gerbner, G. and Gross, L., (1976)).

Multiple repetition of sadism scenes where the hero of the cartoon causes someone pain, evokes a fixation on the aggression in children's mind and promotes the elaboration of similar behavior models. Children imitate what they see on screens, this being a consequence of the identification process. They identify themselves to the being or to the deflected behavior which is not at all punished or even blamed on screens, afterwards they imitate and assimilate this behavior model. In 1970 Albert Bandura was already saying that one television model can become an object of imitation for millions (Bamiduro J.A. (2002)).

During computer games children kill and feel in regards to this a certain satisfaction of mentally violating moral norms. There are practically no human feelings in the virtual world; when they kill someone in their game, children do not feel what usually human being feel: pain, regret, empathy. On the contrary, usual feelings are suppressed and instead of them children enjoy attack and humiliation and the lack of self-restraint. In cartoons the aggression is accompanied by bright and colorful images. Heroes are beautifully dressed or they are in a beautiful place or just a beautiful scene is drawn, followed by murder, fight and other aggressive behavior models; all of these is done to make the cartoon attractive (Carr A. (2000)). If we pour scene of sadism into already existing basis of beauty notions, then the established points of view are simply blurred. In this manner, an aesthetic perception is formed, a new culture of the human. Children are looking forward to seeing these cartoons or films, being perceived as something normal. They have longing for them and do not understand why adults with traditional perceptions of normal and beauty do not give their permission for watching.

It often happens that heroes in cartoons are ugly and have a repulsing appearance. What is this needed for? The issue is that children tend to identify them not only with the behavior of heroes. Children's mechanisms of imitation are responsive and so thin that they are able to detect the least emotional changes or pulled faces. The beast are mean, stupid and crazy. And children identify themselves with such heroes, bringing into correlation their emotions with the beasts' facial expression. After that, they begin to behave in a similar manner: it is not possible to adopt a mean facial expression and remain a good-soul inside, to grin and to tend "gnawing the granite of science", as in the well-known television series "Sesame street" (Rulter M. Taylor. E. (2002)).

The atmosphere of the video market is pierced by killers, oppressors, wizards and other heroes, talking to whom actually would be avoided in the real world. But children see all of these on screens. The children's unconsciousness is not yet protected by wise thinking and by life experience, which permits to delimit the real and the relative. For a child, everything what is seen represents the reality and it is engraved for life. The screen of television with oppressions in adults' world has replaced mothers and grannies, the processes of reading and familiarization with the genuine culture. Hence the growth of emotional and psychic disorders, depressions, teenagers' suicides and unreasonable cruelty of children (Roza. G. Mercy M. (2001)).

The main danger of the television is the suppression of will and consciousness, being similar to the narcotic addiction. The American psychologist A. More says that continuous contemplation of something, tiring eyes, produces hypnotic stiffness, accompanied by the weakening of will and attention. After a certain period of exposure, light flashes, winkling and specific rhythm begin to interact with cerebral alpha-rhythms which are responsible for the concentration of the attention and the following happens: the cerebral rhythmics is disorganized and the syndrome of attention deficit with hyperactivity is developed.

The flow of the seen and heard information, not requiring concentration and mental effort is passively accepted. In time, this attitude is transferred to the real life and the child begins to perceive it in the same manner. And it becomes harder to concentrate on a task, to make a mental or volitional effort. The child gets used to do only those things that do not require any kind of efforts; with difficulty participates in class and apprehends the taught lessons. But without an active mental activity, the development of neural connections, memory and association is not possible. The computer and the television are robbing childhood to children (Ishola AO. (2009)).

Instead of playing active games, experiencing real emotions and feelings and communicating with friends pf the same age and parents, getting to know themselves through the real world surrounding them, children are staying for hours or even full days and nights in front of the computer or the television, depriving themselves from the possibility of evolution, given only in childhood. The media influences people in different ways, some positive and some negative (Baker, R.K. and Ball, S.J., (1969)).

It is important to realize although media can have a positive effect on society too much exposure to television, computers, or magazines can lead to unhealthy effects. The media gives people a way to connect with one another through news updates or even social networking. Most everyone wakes up in the morning grabs the newspaper, computer, or flips on the television to educate themselves on the worldly happenings of that day. According to Manali Oak author of "Positive Effects of the Media". "Research has revealed that media is responsible for influencing a major part of our daily life. Media contribute to a transformation in the cultural and social values of the masses. Media can bring about a change in the attitudes and beliefs of the common man. The persuasive nature of the content presented over media influences the thoughts and behavior of the general public. Media has a direct impact over the lifestyle of society (Gbadeyan R.A. (2008))."

Positive effects of Media: McCombs, M. and Shaw, D. L., (1972); Belson, W., (1967); Roza. G. Mercy M. (2001); Gbadeyan R.A. (2008); Ishola AO. (2009); Rulter M. Taylor. E. (2002)

• The common man gets the latest news within a fraction of seconds. The distance is not at all a barrier now. The news they get through media help them in their daily life a lot.

• The media helps common people to exchange information and it acts as a common platform. The public get knowledge and awake to raise questions, on seeing the news in newspaper and TV.

• The media helps to bring out the hidden talents of the people. The children learn many good things through media.

• By reading newspaper, the children learn many things, their reading habit increases and their vocabulary enhances by learning new words. Their knowledge increases by watching geographical channel, quiz programs and speeches by famous personalities of different fields.

• The cartoon channels make the children happy.

• The games increase their logical thinking power and grasping of things. The attitude, approach and behavior of the common people will also change, when exposed to media.

• The media conducts polls and let public to take part in social issues. Through blogging in the internet and writing letters to the editor in newspapers, many people give voice about their opinion in different political and social matters.

Negative effects of Media (Berkowitz, Leonard, (1964); Gottfredson D. (2001); Noble, G., (1975); Baker, R.K. and Ball, S.J., (1969); The Courier (2001)**):**

• Some bogus news given in the newspaper may raise blood pressure and create negative feelings in the mind.

• Over exposure to media may cause health problems also. The advertisements shown in TV and newspaper have got both positive and negative impact. The children learn violence by seeing movies and TV programs. They imitate super heroes they see in the screen which may cause danger to their life. The overexposure to media make them behave more aggressively, which spoils their future also.

• The children get immense pleasure in playing video games and they spend hours together before computer, surfing through internet. They see both the good and the bad things through media. The parents should make the children to play outdoor games and do physical exercise, diverting their attention from the media.

• The fashion shows, dance and music programs attract youngsters very much. They like to spend money for makeup, clothing and jewels on the influence of models and actors.

• The youngsters wish to take part in these programs, which are unsuitable for many persons.

• The middle aged persons are stuck up with TV serials and show much interest in raising social status, by wasting money.

The media has brought the people all over the world very closer. We have to take the positive aspects and use it for good purpose. The media and public should help to drive away the negative effects of the media.

It was emphasized at the outset that the 'effects' of mass media have to be considered at a level beyond that of the individual audience member and the aggregate of individual behaviors. The path by which collective effects are produced is, in general, simple enough to grasp, but the extent to which effects have occurred resists simple or certain assessment and rarely been the subject of sustained investigation or thought (The Courier (2001)).

As the mass media have developed they have, incontrovertibly, achieved two thins. They have, between them, diverted time and attention from other activities and they have become a channel for reaching more people with more information than was available under 'pre-mass media' conditions. These facts have implications for any other institution which requires allocation of time, attention and the communication of information, especially to large numbers and in large quantities. The media compete with other institutions and they offer ways of reach in continuing institutional objectives. It is this which underlies the process of institutional effect. Other social institutions are under pressure to adapt or respond in some way, or to make their own use of the mass media. In doing so, they are likely to alert, Because this is a slow process, occurring along with other kinds of social change, the specific contribution of the media cannot be accounted for with any certainty.

If this argument is accepted, it sees unlikely that any institution will be unaffected, but most open to change will be those concerned with 'knowledge' in the broadest sense and which are most universal and unselective in their reach. In most societies, this will suggest politics and education as the most likely candidates, religion in some cases and to a lesser degree, legal institution's. In general we would expect work, social services, science, and the military to be only tangentially affected by the availability of mass media. Insofar as we can regard leisure and sport as an institution in modern society this should perhaps be added to politics and education as the most directly interrelated with the mass media.

Children, who observe (in the media or in the environment around them) others exhibiting a specific aggressive behavior, *e.g.* hitting, are more likely to perform the same aggressive behavior immediately.

Exposure to media violence has been positively related to subsequent aggressive behavior, ideas,

arousal, and anger. Additionally, there is a significant negative effect of exposure to violence on subsequent helping behavior. Infrequent exposure is not likely to produce lasting consequences, but parents, particularly need to be urged to protect their children against the kinds of repeated exposures that excessive play with violent video games or immersion in violent TV programs is likely to produce.

(Ray, *et al).* from India reported that children having exposure to violence through media had poorer school performance and its impact on their psychosocial adjustments was detrimental. Another study from India showed that vivid display of violence through media (9/11 terrorist attack) caused stress in adolescents.

(Hopf, *et al)* showed that the more frequently children view horror and violent films during childhood, and the more frequently they play violent electronic games at the beginning of adolescence, the higher will these students' violence and delinquency be at the age of 14.

(Primack, *et al)* showed that excessive TV viewing in adolescence is a risk factor for development of depression in young adulthood. TV viewing may play an exacerbating, if not causal, role in the development of attention-deficit/hyperactivity disorder (ADHD) This hypothesis is consistent with evidence indicating that children with ADHD watch more television than their peers and experience significant impairments in comprehending stories, a crucial skill in achieving academic success.

(While Zimmerman, *et al)* reported that any deleterious longitudinal relation between television and cognitive outcomes may be more salient among children with ADHD, (Acevedo-Polakovich, *et al)* observed no effect. Thus, a more careful examination of the relation between television viewing and children's cognitive abilities are needed.

(Bickham, *et al*)investigated the relationship between TV viewing time, content, context, and peer integration. As children spend more total time watching TV, they spend a significantly shorter amount of time with friends as compared to those who don't. Thus, viewing television causes poor peer relationships and thereby increases the risk for social isolation, anxiety disorder, agoraphobia, and antisocial behavior, including aggression and gang involvement. Some authors found that the more time children spent watching TV, the less time they spent with their families. While TV may isolate children, the reverse causal direction is also plausible – lonely children may turn to TV for entertainment and companionship. Children who are marginalized by their peers use TV to escape the stresses of their lives and meet their social needs. Conversely, children who are socially integrated spend less time watching TV. Thus, it can be argued that it is social isolation that motivates excessive media use. Overall, it is most likely that both effects occur –children who watch more TV become more socially isolated, which leads them to spend more time watching TV. While TV viewing is often perceived as anisolating activity, it frequently occurs in the company of friends. Because socializing builds interpersonal skills, TV viewing with friends may provide a venue for these skills to develop. It is important to consider content whenever investigating the relationships between media use and behaviors. Violent television viewing may influence younger children to be more antisocial; resulting in their becoming socially isolated which, in turn, attracts them to more violent media. To optimize children's social development and long term mental health, parents, teachers, and pediatricians should discourage the viewing of violent television programs. (INDIAN PEDIATRICS 563 VOLUME 47__JULY 17, 2010RAY AND JAT ELECTRONIC MEDIA AND CHILDREN)

Dietz and Gortmaker reported that each additional hour of TV viewing per week increased the risk of obesity by 2%. The experimental study by Robinson found strong evidence of a causal link between TV viewing and children being overweight. In India, this association has also been emphasized.

(Epstein, *et al)* conducted a randomized trial and found that reducing television viewing and computer use may have an important role in preventing obesity and in lowering BMI in young children, and these changes may be related more to changes in energy intake than to changes in physical activity. In the absence of regulations restricting food advertising aimed at children, reduction in television viewing is a promising approach to reducing excess energy intake.

Maccoby and Jacklin (1974) examined gender differences in two types of emotion expressions: frustration reactions (outbursts of negative emotions such as anger or crying in response to frustrating situations) and fear. They reported that infant boys and girls were similar in their frustration reactions but that girls' negative emotional outbursts diminished with age more than boys'. As a result, toddler (18-month-old) boys showed greater frustration reactions than girls. This developmental pattern may reflect a trend for girls to decrease their display of externalizing emotions, such as angry outbursts, because they are acquiring an implicit understanding of society's female gender roles or because of girls' increasing advantage in language and self-regulation abilities in the toddler years. Interestingly, Maccoby and Jacklin reported no consistent gender differences for children's expression of fear Researchers who investigate a cause for the large increase in childhood obesity discovered that there are multifactoral influences contributing to the problem. These included reduced funds for school athletic programs, an increase in the availability of soda and snacks, an explosion of fast-food availability, larger restaurant portions, and a growing number of high- calorie and high-fat products (Rideout, 2004).

Another potential influence to childhood obesity attracting attention is that of the role of media in obesity trends.

Rideout's (2004) testimony summarized the KFF's research in the past 20 years on media and childhood obesity. The KFF's report evaluated research in public health, marketing, media, and childhood development. As early as 1985, Rideout (2004) reported that a study of more than 13,000 children found evidence to suggest that for each additional one hour of TV viewing, there is a 2% increase in childhood obesity. This study adjusted for prior weight, socio-economic status, maternal weight, and race. The KFF (2004) reported a similar relationship in a majority of national studies, suggesting that Displacement Theory may account for the findings.

This review of the literature did not support Displacement Theory as the reason for increased rates of obesity, though logic may suggest otherwise. Rather, Rideout (2004) pointed to TV ads as the possible culprit. Children see' an estimated 40,000 ads annually, most of which are for food (cereal, candy, soda, chips, fast food). With a 2004 food product budget of $10 billion, marketing increasingly focuses on children (KFF, 2004).

Research demonstrated that foods ads strongly correlate to a child's choice of food, how many products they request, and which products they request. Ultimately, these requests have a high rate of success in what parents choose (Rideout, 2004). Rideout's findings supported the Social Learning Theory and the Message Interpretation Process model. Advertisers present popular children's characters, enjoyable games, exciting adventures, and promises of positive outcomes to the target audience and thereby guide food choices..

The National Health and Nutrition Examination Survey included 2964 children ages 4 to 11 years and demonstrated a positive correlation between increased media use and increased adiposity (Anderson, Economos & Must, 2008).

Others have reported similar findings (Henderson, 2007; Anderson, Crespo, Bartlett, Cheskin, & Pratt, 1998; Mendoza, Zimmerman, & Christakis, 2007). The research sought a correlation between weight and children engaged in low levels of physical activity and high levels of sedentary behavior to understand if age, gender, race, and weight effected results.

The Anderson, Economos and Must's (2008) analysis suggested that "a substantial proportion of young children are inadequately active andhigWy sedentary". These two factors likely contribute to childhood obesity rates in the US. A significant higher proportion of obese girl, age 4-11 years, had low levels of physical activity and high sedentary behavior (Anderson, Economos & Must, 2008). Greater media use was associated with an increased likelihood of obesity in pre-adolescent non-Hispanic girls (Anderson, Economos & Must, 2008).

The researchers (Anderson, Economos & Must, 2008) concured with Rideout (2004) thatexposure to food ads encouraged consumption of nutrient poor, high caloric snacks while viewing TV influenced obesity rates. Displacement Theory is controversial since highly sedentary behavior alone does not predict an increase in obesity among all cohorts. The Social Learning Theory and the Message Interpretation model provide an explanation of the Anderson, Economos and Must (2008) findings. The appeal to the 4 to 11 year old TV audience includes role models, topical interest, and socially desirable outcomes, which influence the program choices of children and supports the idea that the Social Learning Theory and the Message Interpretation Process model were at work.

There is compelling evidence that obesity/overweight in children is a global trend that may result from increased sedentary behavior related to increased media use. Wang and Lobstein (2006), the World Health Organization (2000), and the International Obesity Task Force (2004) reported that childhood obesity continues to accelerate in areas of the world where media access has become readily available. Health consequences of obesity in children included hypertension, metabolic syndrome, coronary artery disease, poor self-image, and reduced physical activity tolerance. International studies highlighted the morbidity of childhood obesity and its relationship to media.

A study by Lajous et al. (2009) used a cross-sectional survey of over 13,000 boys and girls ages 11-18 in Morales, Mexico to assess media usage and its correlation

with increased fat mass and distribution. Multivariable regression analysis adjusted for potential cofounders, such as age, sex, and socioeconomic status, correlating the variables with time viewing TV, DVDs, and video games.
Lajous et aI. (2009) found a positive correlation between increased adiposity and increased media use in pre-teen and teen-aged males and pre-menarche females. Increased body mass index (BMI) and fat distribution was greatest among 11-12 year old boys and lowest among sexually mature females. These results compared favorably to others, which found a correlation between obesity and increased media use (Proctor et aI., 2003; Anderson et aI., 1998; Hernandez et al., 1999; Gortmaker et aI., 1996). Lajous et ale (2009) results may be confounded by inaccurate reporting, a lack of a reverse effect of media viewing, and other unrecognized variables. The report underscored the importance of understanding modifiable determinates of adolescent obesity and identifying culturally effective behavior strategies to help shape national public policy.

Kang et aI. (2010) examined the association between media use and metabolic syndrome based in a cross-sectional survey of households with children who participated in the 2005 Korean National Health arid Nutrition Examination Survey. The National C40lesterol Education Program-Adult Treatment Panel III (NCEP-ATP III) defined metabolic syndrome. Over 10,000 households were randomly selected "through a stratified, multistage, probability sampling design that was based on geographical area, sex, and age" (Kang et aI., 2010, p. 73).

A weighted probability of samples allowed for extrapolation of results to the entire Korean population. A
group of cardiometabolic risk factors associated with adult populations including coronary artery disease, hypertension, and metabolic syndrome were associated in children's samples as well. The cluster of risk factors observed in children continues into adulthood (Deitz, 1998; Katzmarzyk et aI., 2001; Srinivasan, Meyers, & Berenson, 2002).

Using quartiles of screen time, Kang et ai. (2010) data revealed that the mean

BMI, waist circumference, blood pressure, total cholesterol and triglyceride levels increased positively as the quartile of media time increased. A negative correlation existed between income and screen time (Kang et al., 2010). The mean media time were higher for the subjects with metabolic syndrome. After adjusting for age, sex, income, and geographic location, subjects who spent 2: 35 hours per week engaged in media activities had an odds ratio of 2.23 for having metabolic syndrome as compared to subjects who spent ~ 16 hours per week (Kang et al., 2010). Media usage is independently associated with metabolic syndrome in Korea (Kang et al., 2010). In addition, the Kang et ai. (2010) data suggested a positive association between metabolic syndrome and increased media time. The prevalence of metabolic syndrome was dose dependent. The Kang and Lajous studies appeared to lend credence to Displacement Theory. As the amount of media usage increases, there are fewer hours in the day for other more physical activities. The greatest adverse health effects on children occurred when media use increased to the point where there was no time left for physical activities. Reports indicated that TV viewing increased meal frequency and intake of energy-dense snack food (Stroebele & Castro, 2004; Philips et al., 2004; Lowry, Weschler, Galuska, Fulton & Kahn, 2002).

As media use increased, readily available snack foods displaced more preparation-intensive healthy foods. Children's blood pressure rates in the US have increased in recent years (Din-Dzietham, Liu, Bielo, & Shamsa, 2007; Muntner, He, Cutler, Wildman, & Whelton, 2004).

Sorof andDaniels (2002) demonstrated an association between obesity and hypertension in children, while Heelan and Eisennlann (2006) reported an association between adiposity and sedentary behaviors, which included media usage. A positive correlation between TV viewing and increased systolic BP was found among Belgian boys ages 6 to 12 (Guillaume, Lapidus, Bjomtorp, & Lambert, 1997).

A novel study by Martinez-Gomez, Tucker, Heelan, Welk, and Eisenmann (2009) examined the effect of sedentary behavior on blood pressure among young children. Martinez- Gomez et al. (2009) recruited 111 participants who wore an accelerometer for seven days to obtain objective measurements of sedentary behavior in children ages 3 to 8 years old. Body composition, anthropometric measurements, and resting blood pressure were obtained. Parents reported the amount of time subjects engaged in sedentary media activities. After controlling for age, sex, height, and adiposity, Martinez-Gomez et aI. (2009) found a positive association between increased blood pressure and increased media usage. Sedentary behavior over all did not correlate with blood pressure, but TV viewing has a significant association with increased blood pressure independent of adiposity. Participants in the lowest tertile of screen use had the lowest blood pressure (Martinez-Gomez et al., 2009).

Martinez-Gomez et aI. (2009) postulatedthat TV viewing and computer use may not have the same metabolic and physiological effects, and they should be considered as separate variables in future research. Displacement Theory and the Message Interpretation Process model appear to be acting upon the forgoing findings. Negative associations between prolonged media use and detrimental outcomes among children are numerous. Associations range from childhood violence (Centerwall, 1994) and aggression (Robinson, Wilde, Navracruz, Haydel, & Varady, 2001) to obesity (Anderson et aI.,1998; Gortmaker et aI., 1996; Hernandez et aI., 1999; Robinson, 1999; Crespo et ai. 2001;Robinson, 1999) and poor school performance (Taras & Potts-Damenta, 2005). The effect of media on children's vision is rarely studied and children often do not seek medical help for their vision complaints.

Bener, Al-Mahdi, Vachhani, AI-Nufal and Ali (2010) aimed to elucidate whether excessive use of media affected vision in school aged children in a developing country.

A cross-sectional study by Bener et ai. (2010) used random sampling to examine 2467children ages 6 to 18 in schools in Qatar. The t-test determined significant differences between two continuous variables. The chi-square and Fisher's exact test determined differences in proportions of riables among groups. To determine differences between group means, the ANOVA test was used.

Bener et ai. (2010) reported significant proportion of students with low vision spent ~ 3 hours per day on the internet. Those cohorts who reported the most time spent. in physical activities had the largest proportion of normal vision. Low vision is "strongly associated with unhealthy lifestyle habits, such as prolonged hours spent on the internet and reclining and having a high BMI" (Bener et al., 2010, p. 384). Physical activities are displaced by media use, which may aid the development of better vision by promoting different functioning of the visual apparatus. It is postulated that the refractive changes that cause myopia may be caused by extensive viewing of near objects during development (Straker, Pollock,&Maslen,2009)

Heim et al. (2007) designed an exploratory study to investigate specific media use in children to determine if psychosocial factors and different types of media use variables were associated. They employed a factor analysis of surveys to measure children's self-concept and media usage. Children evaluated their internal own concept of psychosocial factors and how often they watch TV/videos, play video games, surf the Internet, use chat, or work on their computer. Certain activities were significantly associated with psychosocial factors (Heim et al., 2007).

Children who spent less time on entertainment media scored higher on their perception of scholastic competence than the children who spent more time. This suggested that mastery of difficult technologies increased self-esteem among peers (Heim et al., 2007). However, children with high rates of media *and* Gameboy use scored lower on social acceptance (Heim et al.,2007). Heim et al. (2007) found an association between parental monitoring and usage of media

Heim et ai. (2007) suggested that "when parents are actively involved in their child's daily activities, the child is more likely to embrace media for creative, educational purposes rather than as a medium for games or TV" . In a perspective from the *Department ofPediatrics, Advanced Pediatric Center* in India Ray and Jat (2010) reported that excessive TV use may be a risk factor for development of depression and ADHD. They reported a positive correlation between frequent reading of print media about dieting and weight loss and girls who reported unhappiness about their body weight.

Ray and Jat (2010) suggested that TV impairs peer relationships, and increases the risk for social isolation, anxiety disorder, agoraphobia, ADHD, and antisocial behavior. There was a positive association between viewing media with violent content and increased violent behavior, ideas, and anger (Ray & Jat, 2010). The study reported a negative correlation between violent media viewing and altruistic behaviors (Ray & Jat, 2010).

Hastings et ai. (2009) conducted a study of 70 children ages 6 to 10 via parental report. They sought information concerning the content, amount, and social context (e.g. parental monitoring, with siblings/friends etc.) of children's game playing/computer use and if there is a relationship to child health outcomes. The results of their study were mixed, with the type of media and the amount of time spent with that media largely predictive of positive or negative health outcomes. Educational games provided stress relief, increased attentiveness, school performance, and may increase supportive relationships (Hastings et al., 2009). Recreational games were associated with poor school performance and attention, increased aggressiveness, and externalized behaviors (Hastings et al., 2009). A strong correlation existed between violent video games and aggressive behavior. Hastings et ai. (2009) reported that both positive and negative health outcomes more strongly correlated as the time spent in media activity increases.

This study was limited by a homogenous, small, non-randomized cohort and biased by the use of parental report. In addition, the research represented a snapshot in time and provides no longitudinal information. Displacement Theory is not supported by the findings as increased educational media time correlated negatively to behavior problems. The Social Learning Theory and the Message Interpretation Process model may explain the results. For example, identification with violent game characters may increase propensity toward externalized behaviors. Jackson, Brown and Pardun (2008) examined the association between risky health behaviors, media, and a TV in the bedroom. The study applied multivariable analysis to a detailed media use survey, which was completed by 1,200 participants from 14 public schools in the southeastern us. Variables included, but were not limited to having a TV in the bedroom, frequency of TV viewing, identification with actors, parental oversight, mature content programming, ~tiation of smoking and sexual intercourse. Respondents reported the least happiness and increased loneliness when viewing TV in the bedroom. A positive correlation existed between time spent TV viewing and identification with characters (Jackson, Brown, & Pardun, 2009).

Jackson et ale (2009) reported that for white males there was a 3.5 times greater likelihood of initiation of smoking and a 2 times greater likelihood of initiation of sexual intercourse when a TV is in the bedroom. However, parental oversight appeared to moderate these negative health outcomes (Jackson et aI., 2009). The Social Learning Theory and the Message Interpretation Process nlodel support these results. If children positively identify with TV characters, it may have promoted risky health behaviors, especially if realistic consequences were ignored. Displacement Theory may account for feelings of unhappiness and loneliness; TV isolated an individual and displaced social interactions.

Wilson (2008) reviewed evidence of the link between media use and children's emotions, and explored how media affects social development. She analyzed over 110 articles published between 1963 and 2007. Her report revealed a good deal of evidence to suggest that media contributed to children's fear and anxiety especially in younger children. Those who viewed TV 2: 6 hours per day were more likely to have anxiety, depression, and PTSD. There was strong evidence of a positive correlation between violent TV programs and video games with aggressive behavior (Wilson, 2008). However, Wilson (2008) found that educational programs and situation comedy targeted to youth increased altruism, cooperation, and tolerance.

Wilson (2008) demonstrated that media effect "depends on the content to which the children are exposed", and is highly influenced by age, gender, race, home life, and temperament. Children's choice of media, identification with characters, modeling of behavior, and imprinting may the mechanisms by which children's behaviors were acquired. This lends support to Social Learning Theory and the Message Interpretation Process model.

Lieberman and So (2009) selected studies on media and learning completed on children ages 3 to 6 to assess the link that different media had on children's acquisition of skills for language, thinking, reading, mathematics, creativity, and collaboration.

Similarly, Hisrich and Blanchard's (2009) literature review discussed the effects of digital media use and emergent literacy skills. Both teams reported a body of research that demonstrated numerous beneficial cognitive effects of digital media when well designed computer, TV, and game programs were utilized. Digital media can increase group interaction, collaboration, and motivation (Hisrich & Blanchard, 2009; Lieberman & So, 2009). Educational TV programs were associated with better school entry skills (Hisrich & Blanchard, 2009). Both studies reported a lasting positive effect of educational programs. Lieberman and So (2009) were unable to determine which form of media instruction is most effective, or isolate the reasons why ne fonn is more effective than another. Hisrich and Blanchard (2009) suggested that media exerted a largely unknown influence on children's cognition. Most studies to date have been done with small numbers of children over ashort period of time. These limitation hamper the conclusions of Liebennan and So (2009) and Hisrich and Blanchard (2009). Displacement Theory predicts that replacing ad hoc media use with well-designed video games, TV programs, and computer software, children's psychosocial and cognitive outcomes may improve.

Hofferth (2010), Jolin and Weller (2011), and Shen and Williams (2010) all reported atleast some detrimental psychosocial and academic effects of increased media use. Hofferth(2010) and Shen and Williams (2010) found that increased loneliness was associated with increased time spent on line, though the effect may be dependent upon context and personality. For· every one-hour increase in watching TV, there was an association with an increase in depression (Jolin & Weller, 2011). The more time spent on media activities translated to less time spent with parents, siblings, and peers (Hofferth, 2010; Jolin & Weller, 2011; Shen &Williams, 2010), and a decreased sense of community (Shen & Williams, 2010). Poor self-esteem and social incompetence are reported by subjects who spent the greatest amount of time with media (Jolin & Weller, 2011; Shen & Williams, 2010).

Hofferth (2010) found non association between increased media use and behavior problems, but Jolin and Weller (2011)reported an association with decreased attention, especially for TV viewing among 1 and 3 year olds.

Jolin and Weller (2010) reported that 14 year olds who spent more than 3 hours per day with media correlated with greater academic failure and negative school attitudes.

Hofferth's (2010) study found an association between increased video game play and academic failure.Hofferth (2010) and Shen and Williams, (2010) reported some equivocal results with association.

Swing et al. (2010) results concured with other studies that found an association between TV/video and attention problems/attention deficit hyperactivity disorder diagnosis, poorer executive function and proactive cognitive control (Bailey, West, & Anderson, 2010; Bioulac, Arfi & Bouvard, 2008; Mistry, Minkovitz, Strobino & Borzekowski, 2007).

The Displacement Theory, Message Interpretation Process model, and Social Learning Theory are not useful to explain these results. A theory, which accounts for rapid changes of focus, inherent in media, and its relationship to development, would help to explain the Swing findings. Media research studies on children and health outcomes can have different or equivocal findings.

Olson, Kutner and Warner (2010) completed a qualitative study, which used focus groups to ascertain information regarding high school boys feelings about violent video games. Participants made distinctions between the real world and the game world (Olson, Kutner & Warner, 2010).

A positive association between video game play and group cooperation, self-esteem, creative thinking, and problem solving, and a negative correlation between game play and isolation are reported. They hypothesize that violent game play served the same function as rough and tumble play.

Olson, Kutner and Warner (2010) found that boys' use of violent games regulates their emotions and perhaps reduced stress and real-life fighting. The Message Interpretation Process model can be applied to the study results as the participants were more attracted to violent content due to fantasies of power and fame, challenge, coping with anger and stress, and sociability. In addition, the boys are aware that game actions have very different consequences in the real world. The cohorts applied both logical and emotional responses and logical comparisons in their feelings and choices about video games.

Olson et al. (2009) examined 1,254 seventh and eighth grade students to find potential links between problem behaviors and tinle spent with violent video games. Exposure to mature-rated games was a significant predictor of engaging in bullying and aggression, and strongest among girls (Olson et aI. 2009).
The odds of these behaviors increased with the dose of exposure (Olson et aI. 2009). However, there was no association with M-rated games and being the victim of bullies or engaging in delinquent behaviors (Olson et aI. 2009). The Social Learning Theory can be used to predict the above results via repeated imprinting and internalization of aggressive and violent behavior.
In light of the literature revived it can be derived that the studies carried out so far by different investigators are largely on different type of samples.

CHAPTER- 3

METHODOLOGY

Purpose

The theoretical foundation and research investigations raise certain questions regarding the effect of Mass Media ,gender, Domicile Status on Cognitive, Social and Emotional Development of Primary School children.

Aims

1. To study the main and interactive effect of mass media on Cognitive, Social and Emotional Development of Primary School children.
2. To study the main and interactive effect of Gender on Cognitive, Social and Emotional Development of Primary School children.
3. To study the main and interactive effect of Status on Cognitive, Social and Emotional Development of Primary School children .

Hypothesis

1. Mass media will have significant main effect on Cognitive, Social and Emotional Development of Primary School children.
2. Gender will have significant main effect on Cognitive, Social and Emotional Development of Primary School children .
3. Domicile Status will have significant main effect on Cognitive, Social and Emotional Development of Primary School children .
4. Mass media and Gender will have significant interactive effect on Cognitive, Social and Emotional Development of Primary School children .
5. Gender and Domicile status will have significant interactive effect on Cognitive, Social and Emotional Development of Primary School children .
6. Mass media and Domicile Status will have significant interactive effect on Cognitive, Social and Emotional Development of Primary School children.
7. Mass media Gender and Domicile status will have significant interactive effect on Cognitive, Social and Emotional Development of Primary School children .

Variables

The variables under the study were:-

1. Independent variables

   Mass Media (TV and Internet)

   Gender (Boys and Girls)

   Domical status (Urban and Rural)

2. Dependent variable-

   Cognitive Development

   Social Development

   Emotional Development

Research design

So as to find the objective answer to the research problem a 2x2x2 factorial design will be adopted to access the variance contributed by each factor. The three independent factors Mass Media (TV and Internet), Gender (Boys and Girls) and Domical status (Urban and Rural) will employed for post – hoc analysis to see their main and interactive effects on cognitive, social and emotional development of the primary school children. It will be labeled as 2x2x2 equal cell frequency design.

2x2x2 Factorial Design

		Mass Media			
		Internet		TV	
		Rural	Urban	Rural	Urban
Gender	Boys	N = 20			
	Girls				

A1 is Mass Media (Internet).

A2 is Mass Media (TV).

B1 is Boys.

B2 is Girls.

C1 is Rural .

C2 is Urban.

AxBxC

Sample-

A random sample of 320 primary school children (age range 6-11 years) with balanced number of Boys and Girls equally from rural and urban nt schools , Jaipur will be taken for further investigation.

The following school shows the distribution of the sample

1	J.J.Public Senior Secondary School , Itawa , Phulera
2	Raj Public Senior Secondary School , Khirva , Phulera
3	Sanskar Public Secondary School , Kaladera , Chomu
4	Green Park Public Senior Secondary School Ghinoi
5	New Tagore Higher Secondary School, Samod
6	Sunil Bal High Secondary School, Bagru
7	Madhmik Balika Adarsh Vidya Mandir, Kishan garh , Renwal
8	Brahmchari Shri Rama Madhmik Vidyalaya, Jamdoli
9	Janta Balika Higher Secondary School, Azad Marg, C-Scheme, Jaipur
10	Veer Balika Higher Secondary School , Kundigar Bheruji ka Rasta , Johri Bazar , Jaipur
11	Disney land Public Higher Secondary School, Malviya Nagar, Jaipur
12	Rawat Bal Vidya Niketan Higher Secondary School, Vivek Vihar, New Sanganer Road, Jaipur
13	Maheshwari Balika Higher Secondary School , Chaura Rasta, Jaipur
14	Surendra Bal Bharti Higher Secondary School , Jaipur
15	St. Joseph Higher Secondary School , Barkat Nagar, Jaipur
16	Tagore Bal Mandir Higher Secondary School, Shastri Nagar , Jaipur
17	Rajputana Green Land Senior Secondary School , Mansarovar, Jaipur
18	Nav Bharti High Secondary School , Ramnagar , Sodala , Jaipur

Controls

1. Only those subjects were included who fulfilled the purpose of the study.
2. Children were at least 6-11 years.
3. Children belonged government schools will be taken for investigation.
4. Children belong to Rural and urban area.

DESCRIPTION OF DIFFERENT TESTS

A. Personal data sheet

It was prepared by the researcher to collect information about demographic variable like age, education, income and marital status.

B. Mass media (TV& Internet)

Mass media Non standardized test used in this research work was developed by self. In the present test 3 alternative responses have been given to each statement i. e. either Agree , Disagree or middle way. The scale consisted 30 items. Including 17 positive items & 13 negative items. Scoring of positive items is 2,1,0, and of negative is 0,1,2.

C. Multifactor emotional intelligence scale

The MEIS—Indian version is also an adaptation of MEIS appropriate for Indian population (Vinod kumar Shanwal, 2003; 2004). It consists of 141 item scale and 31 stimuli designed to measure the following four branches of emotional intelligence (a) perceiving emotions (b) using emotions to facilitate thought (c) understanding emotions (d) managing emotions .

Different components, Stimuli and item of the Indian version of MEIS

S.NO	Components and Sub –Scales	Stimuli	Items
1.	**Identification of Emotions**	**10**	**50**
	Faces	5	25
	Stories	5	25
2.	**Assimilation of Emotions**	**7**	**57**
	Synesthesia	4	36
	Felling Biases	3	21
3.	**Understanding of Emotions**	**12**	**25**
	Blends	4	4

	Progression Transition Relativity	5 2 1	5 12 4
4.	**Regulation of Emotions**	**2**	**9**
	TOTAL	**31**	**141**

D. Social skills check list

It was developed by Madhu Mathur & Saroj Aurora .The checklist was devised to measure social skills in children from childhood through early adolescents (8 to 15 years). The social skills checklist assesses social behaviors on 6 dimensions viz. presentation skill (7 items), Interaction skills (5 items),Conversation (14 items) ,Social integration (14 items), Attitude towards other children (9 items) and attitude towards adults (13 items).Initially 150 items were listed out and given to 10 psychologists for internal consistency and content validity. A pilot study was also carried out and there after only 62 items were retained, which were rated on a three point scale.

E. Cognitive capabilities test

The data were collected with the help of standardized test of cognitive development. cognitive development level were assessed through a test developed by Dr. Vasundhara Padmanbhan. This test is for assessing the cognitive capabilities of primary children. It consists of twenty five cognitive capabilities tasks fitting into the ten schemes of though representational of the transition period from concrete operational to formal operational stage. For the sake of convenience in administration, the test has been divided into three parts, each of which has to be administered on three separate days of a week in order to avoid fatigue. Piaget s model of cognitive development characterized by sequential stages offers an effective liaison between the developmental nature of the child and curriculum of the school.

Scoring

After administering different tests on the different development of Children ,the data were analysed. The raw score for each tests was calculated as per the scoring norms given in the manual. Cognitive, social and Emotional Development as dependent variable While the rest of variables have been treated as independent variables.

Statistical Analysis

Descriptive Statistics along with a 2 x 2 x 2 (ANOVA) with equal cell frequency will be computed through SPSS 17.0 to see the effects of Mass Media, Gender and Domicile Status on Cognitive, Social and Emotional Development of Primary School Children.

CHAPTER- 4

RESULTS

STATISTICAL EVALUATION OF PSYCHOLOGICAL OBSERVATIONS

Observations collected on the psychological variables was statistically analyzed and presented under the following sections:

1.Arithmetic mean (X)

It is calculated to measure the central tendency of parameter which is the 'typical value' in the distribution of particular parameter. All the individual values of the variables are added and then the sum divided by the total number of individuals.

$$X = \frac{\sum X}{N}$$

Where X = mean value

$\sum X$ = Sum of all individual values

N = Number of individuals.

2. Standard Deviation (S.D.)

Standard deviation is a measure of the variation and is universally used to show the scatter of individual measurements around the mean of all the measurement in a given distribution. By definition, it is the square root of the average of the scattered deviations of the measurement from their mean. It is calculated as follows:

$$S.D. = \sqrt{\frac{\sum (X - \bar{X})^2}{N - 1}}$$

Where X = Observed variable

N = Number of individuals

X - X = Deviation from the arithmetic mean.

3. Test of significance - t test

The value of 't' was obtained by applying the following formula:

$$'T' = \frac{\bar{X}_1 - \bar{X}_2}{S} \sqrt{\frac{(N_1 \times N_2}{(N_1 + N_2}}$$

Where S = $\sqrt{\frac{(N_1 - 1)\ V1 + (N_2 - 1)\ V_2}{N_1 + N_2 - 2}}$

Where S was combined standard deviation of two groups X_1 and X_2 means. N_1 and N_2 are number of subject for the respective group.
V_1 and V_2 are variances.

4. ANOVA

The two-way ANOVA compares the mean differences between groups that have been split on two independent variables (called factors). The primary purpose of a two-way ANOVA is to understand if there is an interaction between the two independent variables on the dependent variable. The interaction term in a two-way ANOVA informs you whether the effect of one of your independent variables on the dependent variable is the same for all values of your other independent variable (and vice versa).

The three-way ANOVA is used to determine if there is an interaction effect between three independent variables on a continuous dependent variable (i.e., if a three-way interaction exists). As such, it extends the two-way ANOVA, which is used to determine if such an interaction exists between just two independent variables (i.e., rather than three independent variables).

The observations was analyzed using mean, S.D. ,t test and ANOVA . The summary observation was presented vide table 1 to 21 infra:

TABLE- 1

Statistical comparison between Media (TV & Internet) on Cognitive capabilities test of Primary School Children

Group	N	Mean	SD	S.E.E.	M.D	T-test
TV	160	79.48	16.81	1.33	6.05	3.59
Internet	160	85.53	13.04	1.03		

- Significant at .05 level of significance t .05(318) =1.97

According to table No. 4.1, which indicates that Mean & S.D &S.E.E. of Internet Vs TV group Cognitive capabilities test of Primary School Children i.e. Internet group are 79.48±16.81;1.33, TV group are 85.53±13.04;1.03. As per the table the mean difference of TV Vs Internet group is (6.05) and the t-test was statistically significant as the obtained value (3.59) is less than the tabulated value (1.97) required for t-test to be significant at .05 level of confidence.

Fig -1 Showing Graphical Presentation of **Media (TV & Internet) on Cognitive capabilities test** of Primary School Children

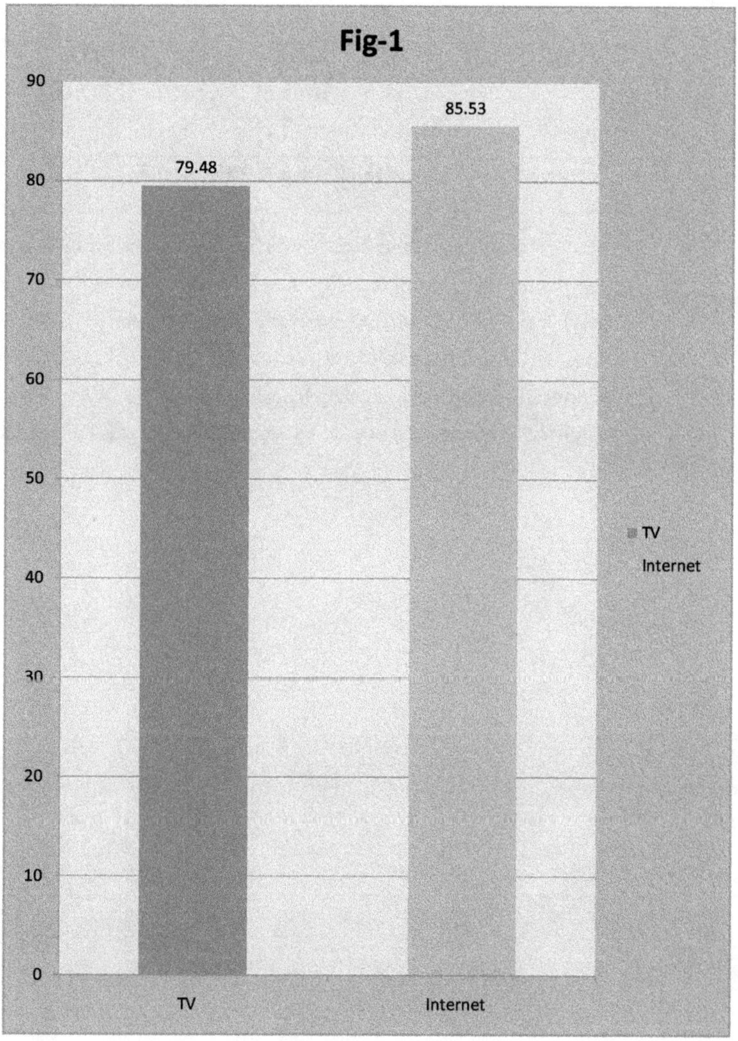

TABLE- 2

Statistical comparison between media (TV & internet) on social skills checklist of primary school children

Group	N	Mean	SD	S.E.E.	M.D.	T-test
TV	160	101.81	12.64	1.00	1.68	1.19
Internet	160	100.13	12.60	1.00		

- Significant at .05 level of significance t .05(318) =1.97

According to table No. 2, which indicates that Mean & S.D &S.E.E. of TV Vs Internet on Social skills checklist of Primary School Children , i.e. TV group are 101.81±12.64;1.00, Internet group are 100.13±12.60;0.99. As per the table the mean difference of TV Vs Internet group is (1.68) and the t-test was statistically insignificant as the obtained value (1.19) is less than the tabulated value (1.97) required for t-test to be significant at .05 level of confidence.

Fig -2 Showing Graphical Presentation of **media (TV & internet) on** social skills checklist of primary school children

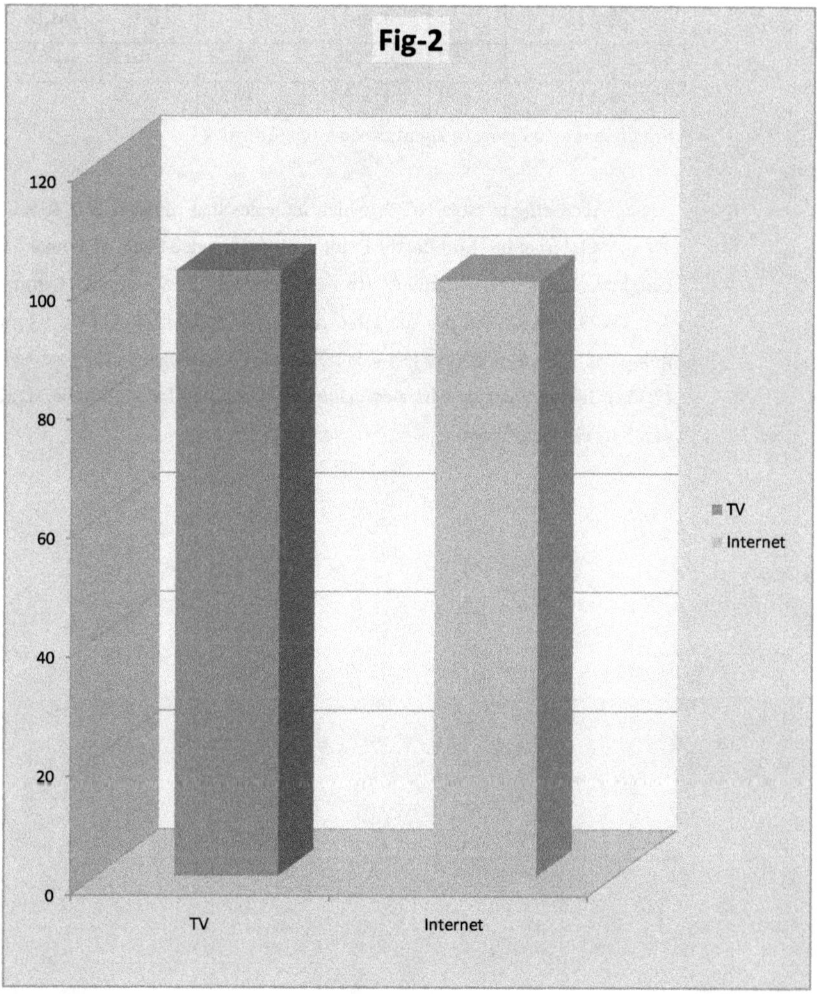

TABLE- 3

Statistical comparison between media (TV & internet) on multifactor emotional intelligence scale of primary school children

Group	N	Mean	SD	S.E.E.	M.D.	T-test
TV	160	495.56	78.23	6.18	63.22	7.15
Internet	160	432.34	79.89	6.32		

- Significant at .05 level of significance t .05(318) =1.97

According to table No. 3, which indicates that Mean & S.D & S.E.E. of TV Vs Internet on Multifactor Emotional intelligence Scale of Primary School Children, i.e. TV group are 495.56±78.23;6.18 Internet group are 432.34±79.89;6.32. As per the table the mean difference of TV Vs Internet group is (63.22) and the t-test was statistically significant as the obtained value (7.15) is higher than the tabulated value (1.97) required for t-test to be significant at .05 level of confidence.

Fig -3 Showing Graphical Presentation of **media (TV & internet) on multifactor emotional intelligence scale of** primary school children

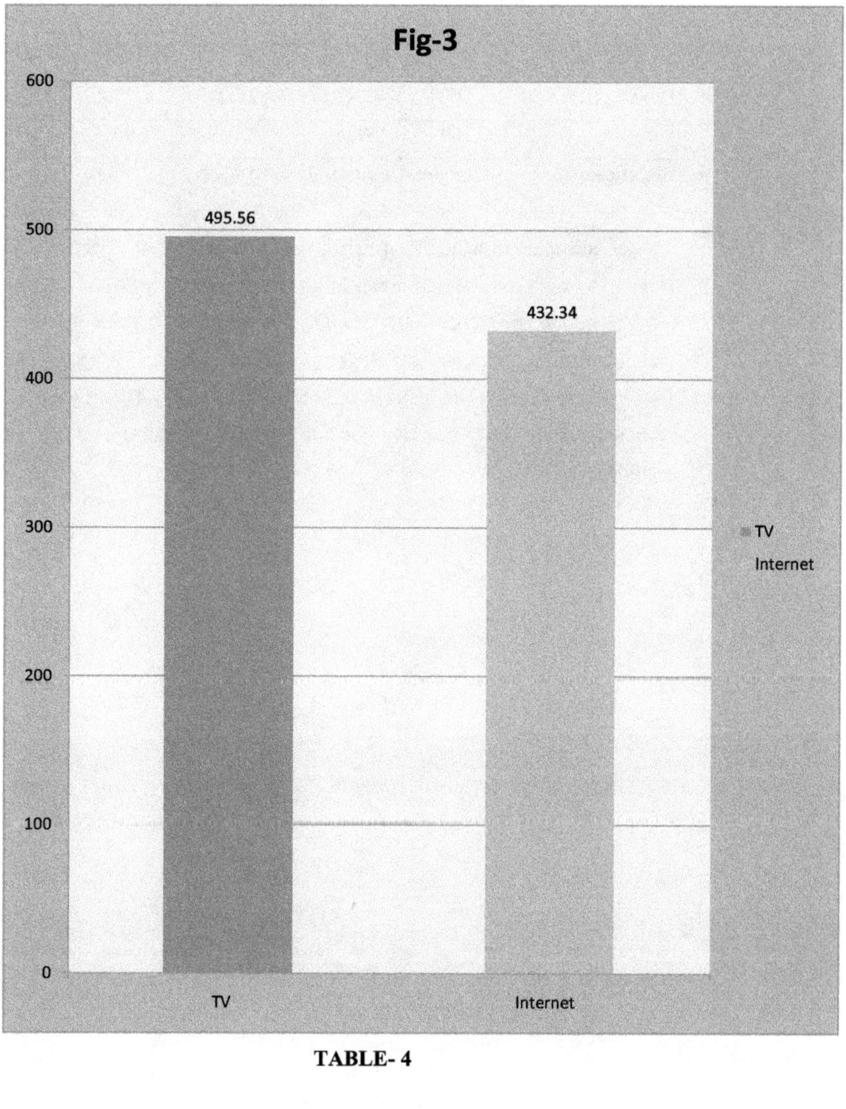

TABLE- 4

Statistical comparison between Gender (Boys Vs Girls) on Cognitive capabilities test of Primary School Children

Group	N	Mean	SD	S.E.E.	M.D	T-test
Boys	160	73.42	17.01	1.34	5.93	3.84
Girls	160	79.35	12.69	1.00		

- Significant at .05 level of significance t .05(318) =1.97

According to table No. 4, which indicates that Mean & S.D &S.E.E. of Boys Vs Girls on Cognitive capabilities test of Primary School Children , i.e. Boys group are 73.42±17.01;1.34, Girls group are 79.35±12.69;1.00. As per the table the mean difference of Boys Vs Girls group is (5.93) and the t-test was statistically significant as the obtained value (3.84) is higher than the tabulated value (1.97) required for t-test to be significant at .05 level of confidence.

Fig -4 Showing Graphical Presentation of **Gender (Boys Vs Girls) on Cognitive capabilities test** of Primary School Children

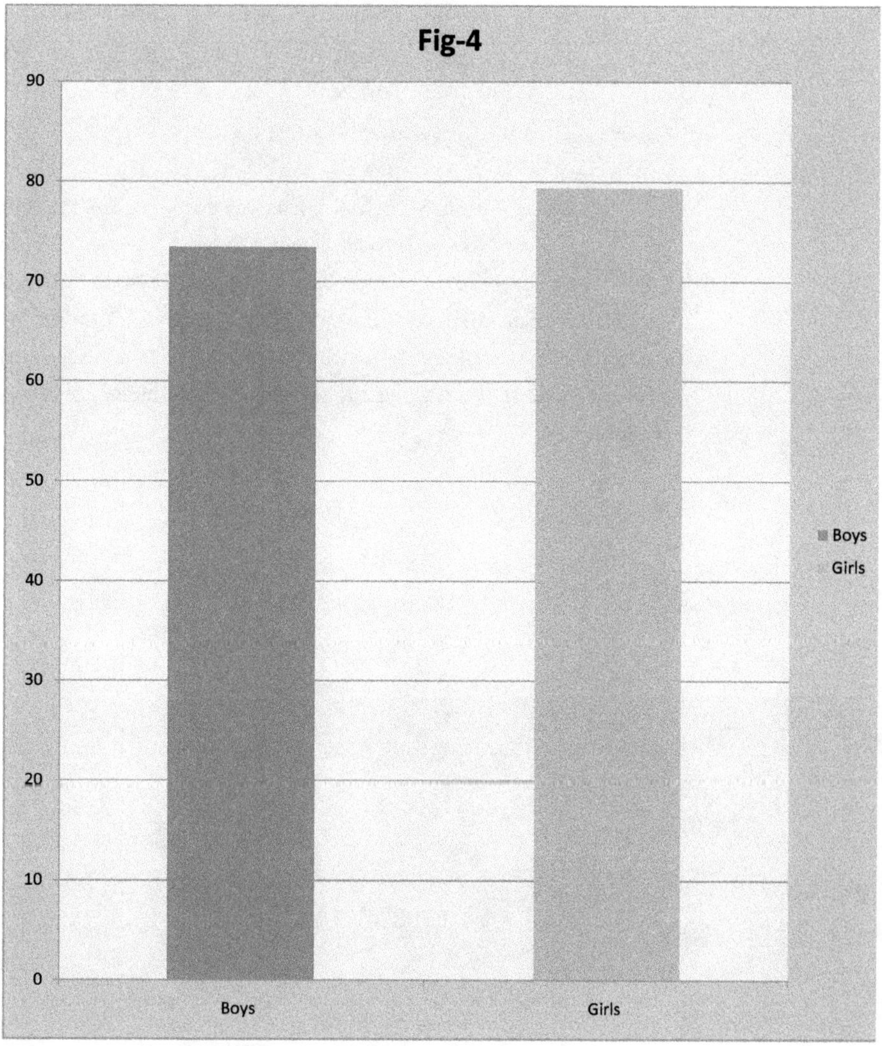

TABLE- 5

Statistical comparison between Gender (Boys Vs Girls) on Social skills checklist of Primary School Children

Group	N	Mean	SD	S.E.E.	M.D.	T-test
Boys	160	99.20	11.68	0.92	3.54	2.53
Girls	160	102.74	13.31	1.05		

- Significant at .05 level of significance t .05(318) =1.97

According to table No. 5, which indicates that Mean & S.D &S.E.E. of Boys Vs Girls on Social skills checklist of Primary School Children , i.e. Boys group are 99.20±11.68;0.92, Girls group are 102.74±13.31;1.05. As per the table the mean difference of Boys Vs Girls group is (3.54) and the t-test was statistically significant as the obtained value (2.53) is higher than the tabulated value (1.97) required for t-test to be significant at .05 level of confidence.

Fig -5 Showing Graphical Presentation of **Gender (Boys Vs Girls)** **on** Social skills checklist of Primary School Children

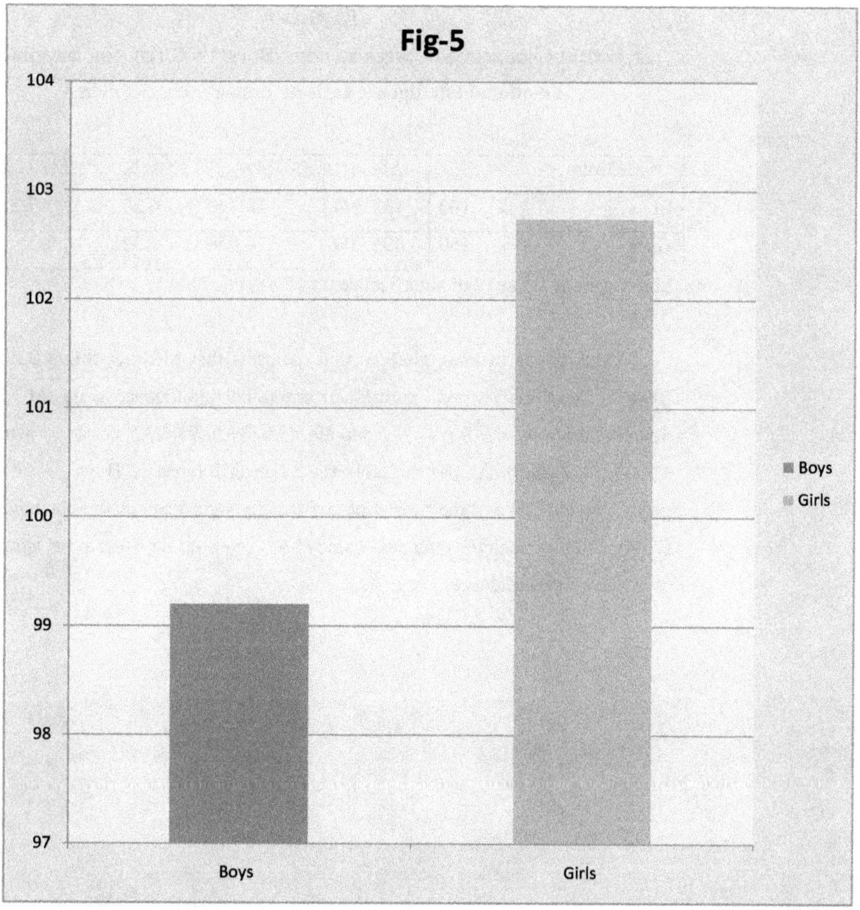

TABLE- 6

Statistical comparison between Gender (Boys Vs Girls) on multifactor emotional intelligence scale of primary school children

Group	N	Mean	SD	S.E.E.	M.D.	T-test
Boys	160	432.694	78.449	6.202	63.21	7.05
Girls	160	495.200	79.956	6.321		.

- Significant at .05 level of significance t .05(318) =1.97

According to table No.6, which indicates that Mean & S.D &S.E.E. of Boys Vs Girls on multifactor emotional intelligence scale of Primary School Children , i.e. Boys group are 495.18±79.94;6.32, Girls group are 432.71±78.48;6.20. As per the table the mean difference of Boys Vs Girls group is (63.21) and the t-test was statistically significant as the obtained value (7.05) is higher than the tabulated value (1.97) required for t-test to be significant at .05 level of confidence.

Fig -6 Showing Graphical presentation of **Gender (Boys Vs Girls) on multifactor emotional intelligence scale of** primary school children

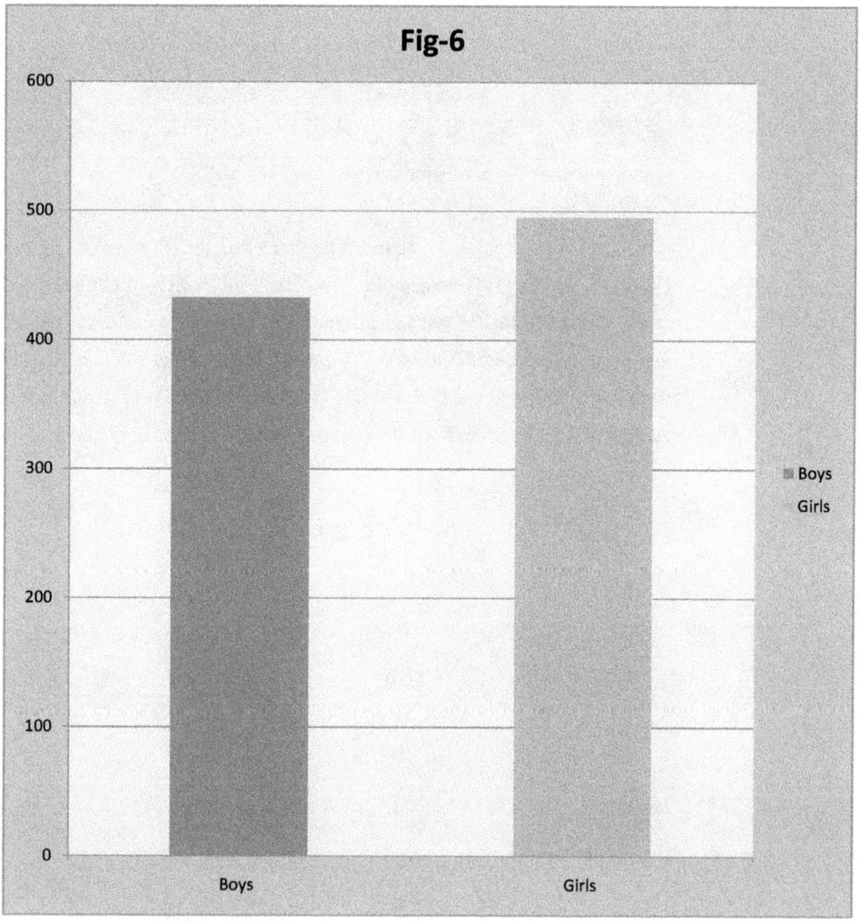

TABLE- 7

Statistical comparison between Domicile (Rural & Urban) on Cognitive capabilities test of Primary School Children

Group	N	Mean	SD	S.E.E.	M.D	T-test
Rural	160	81.91	16.17	1.28	1.17	0.69
Urban	160	83.09	14.45	1.14		

- Significant at .05 level of significance t .05(318) =1.97

According to table No.7, which indicates that Mean & S.D & S.E.E. of Rural Vs Urban on Cognitive capabilities test of Primary School Children i.e. Rural group are 81.91±16.17;1.28, Urban group are 83.09±14.45;1.14. As per the table the mean difference of Rural Vs Urban group is (1.17) and the t-test was statistically insignificant as the obtained value (0.69) is lower than the tabulated value (1.97) required for t-test to be significant at .05 level of confidence.

Fig -7 Showing Graphical presentation of **Domicile (Rural & Urban) on Cognitive capabilities test of Primary School Children**

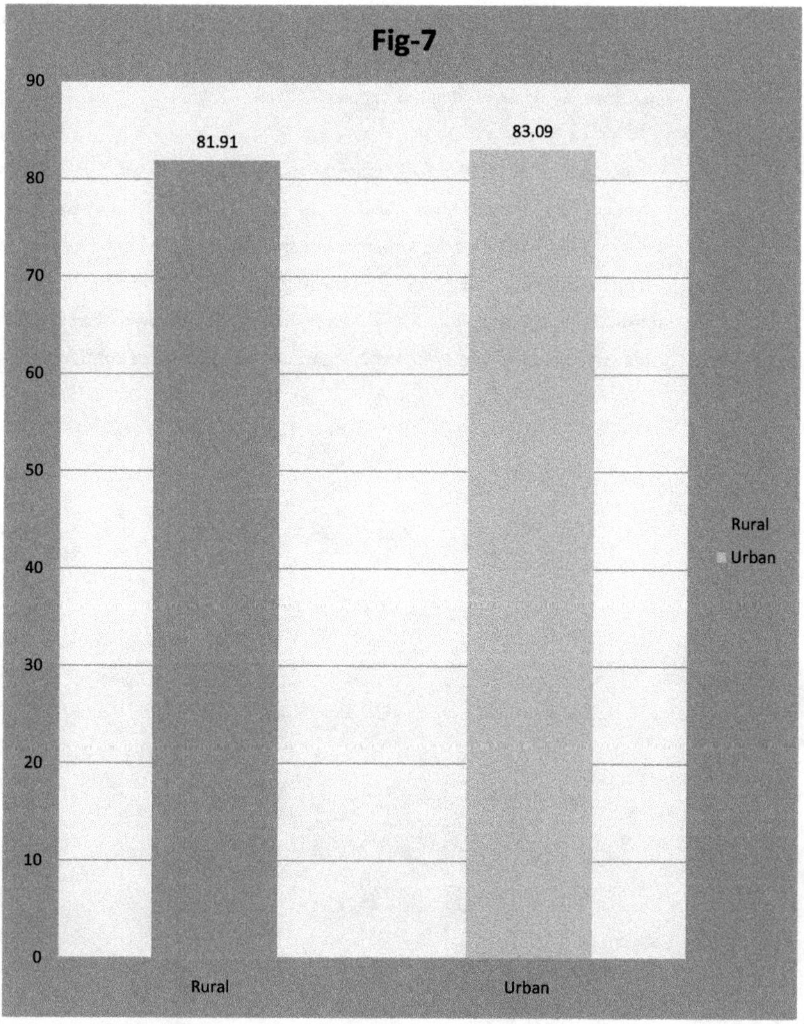

TABLE- 8

Statistical comparison between Domicile (Rural & Urban) on Social skills checklist of Primary School Children

Group	N	Mean	SD	S.E.E.	M.D.	T-test
Rural	160	99.67	12.35	0.98	2.60	1.85
Urban	160	102.28	12.80	1.01		

- Significant at .05 level of significance t .05(318) =1.97

According to table No.8, which indicates that Mean & S.D & S.E.E. of Rural Vs Urban on Social skills checklist of Primary School Children, i.e. Rural group are 99.67±12.35;0.98, Urban group are 102.27±12.80;1.01. As per the table the mean difference of Rural Vs Urban group is (2.60) and the t-test was statistically insignificant as the obtained value (1.85) is lower than the tabulated value (1.97) required for t-test to be significant at .05 level of confidence.

Fig -8 Showing Graphical presentation of **Domicile (Rural & Urban)** **ON** Social skills checklist of Primary School Children

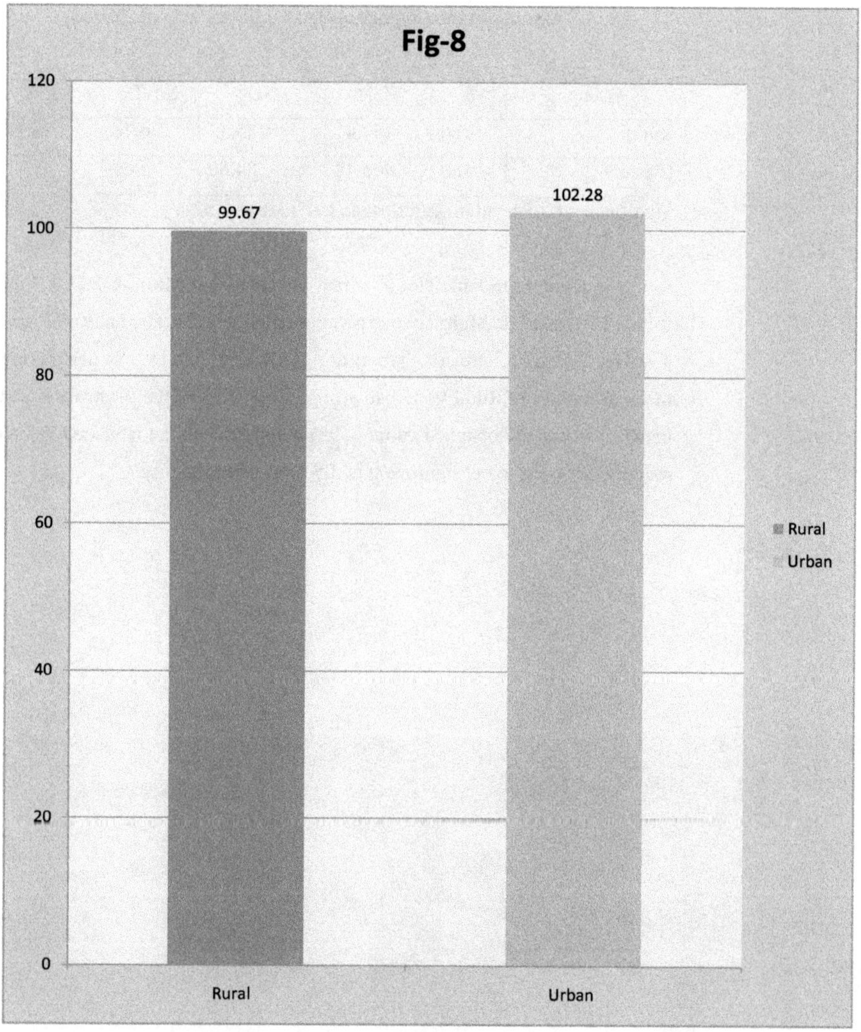

TABLE.9

Statistical comparison between Domicile (Rural & Urban) on multifactor emotional intelligence scale of primary school children

Group	N	Mean	SD	S.E.E.	M.D.	T-test
Rural	160	459.41	85.52	6.76	9.07	0.95
Urban	160	468.48	84.60	6.69		

- Significant at .05 level of significance t .05(318) =1.97

According to table No. 9, which indicates that Mean & S.D & S.E.E. of Rural Vs Urban on Multifactor emotional intelligence scale, i.e. Rural group are 459.41±85.52;6.76, Urban group are 468.48±84.60;6.69. As per the table the mean difference of Rural Vs Urban group is (9.07) and the t-test was statistically insignificant as the obtained value (0.95) is lower than the tabulated value (1.97) required for t-test to be significant at .05 level of confidence.

Fig -9 Showing Graphical presentation of Domicile (Rural & Urban) on **multifactor emotional intelligence scale of** primary school children

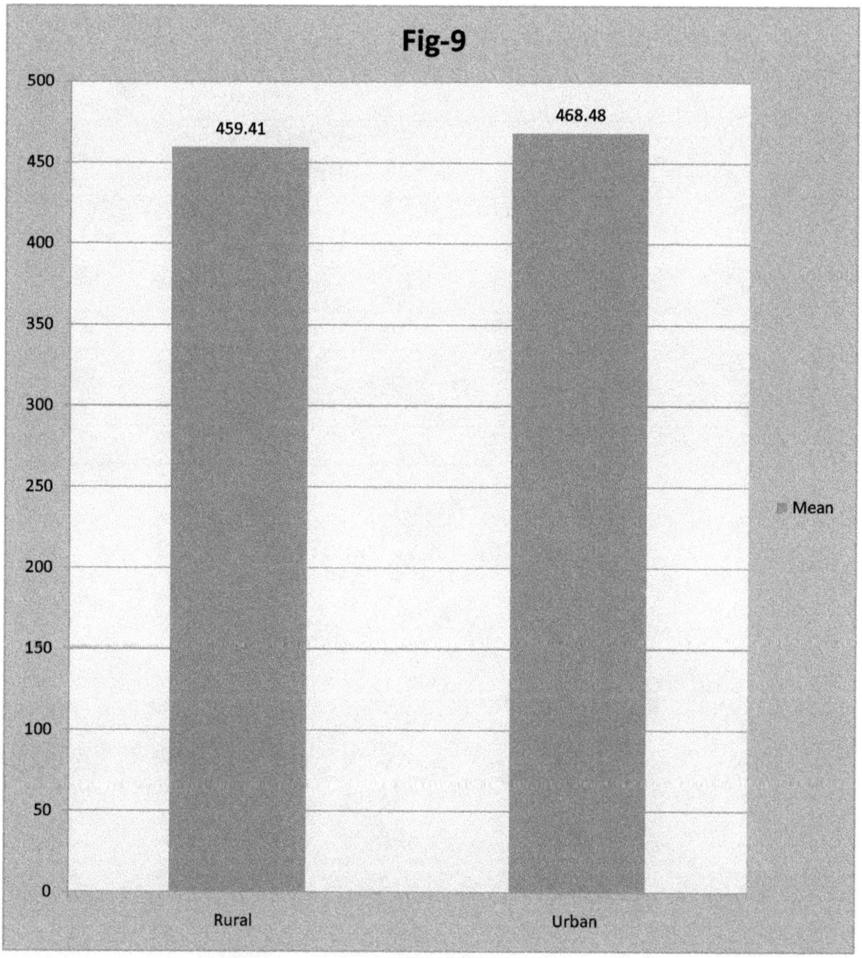

Table-10

(i) **Means of Cognitive capabilities test of Primary School of** Mass Media and Gender Status group

	Cat	**Cognitive capabilities test**	
		Mean	N
TV	Boys	84.17	18
	Girls	78.88	142
	Total	79.48	160
Internet	Boys	85.84	142
	Girls	83.06	18
	Total	85.53	160
Total	TV	85.65	160
	Internet	79.35	160
	Total	82.50	320

Table-10(a)

(ii) 2x2 Analysis of Variance of **Cognitive capabilities test** of Primary School Children of Mass media and Gender Status group

Source of Variation	Sum of Squares	Df	Mean Square	F	Sig.
Mass Media (Internet & TV)	2928.2	1	2928.2	12.95742	Sig
Gender (Boys & Girls)	520.0379	1	520.0379	2.301192	N.S
2-Way Interaction Mass Media (Internet & TV) & gender(Boys & Girls)	50.07825	1	50.07825	0.221599	N.S.
Residual	71411.68	316	225.9863		
Total	74910	319	234.8276		

* Significant at .05 level 'F' value at .05, (1,316)= 3.87

Table-10(a) pertaining to Cognitive capabilities test of Primary School Children response of total sample reveals that:-

i. There is significant effect of Mass media on Cognitive capabilities test of Primary School Children (F=12.95742,P=Sig.)

ii. There is no significant effect of Gender on Cognitive capabilities test of Primary School Children (F=2.301192,P=N.S.)

iii. There is no significant effect of Mass media and Gender group on Cognitive capabilities test of Primary School Children (F=0.221599,P=N.S.).

Table-11

(i) Means of Social skills checklist of Primary School Children of Mass media and Gender Status group

		Social skills checklist	
		Mean	N
TV	Boys	100.83	18
	Girls	101.94	142
	Total	101.81	160
Internet	Boys	98.91	142
	Girls	109.78	18
	Total	100.13	160
Total	TV	99.13	160
	Internet	102.82	160
	Total	100.97	320

Table-11(a)

(ii) 2x2 Analysis of variance of social skills checklist of primary school children of mass media and gender Status group

Source of Variation	Sum of Squares	Df	Mean Square	F	Sig.
Mass Media (Internet & TV)	226.1281	1	226.1281	1.46626	N.S.
Gender (Boys & Girls)	1144.956	1	1144.956	7.424123	Sig
2-Way Interaction Mass Media (Internet & TV) & gender (Boys & Girls)	761.8122	1	761.8122	4.939742	Sig.
Residual	48733.85	316	154.221		
Total	50866.75	319	159.4569		

* Significant at .05 level 'F' value at .05, (1,316)= 3.87

Table-11(a) pertaining to Social skills checklist of Primary School Children response of total sample reveals that:-

i. There is no significant effect of Mass media on Social skills checklist of Primary School Children (F=1.46626,P=N.S.).

ii. There is significant effect of Gender Social skills checklist of Primary School Children (F=7.424123,P=Sig.).

iii. There is significant effect of Mass media and Gender group Social skills checklist of Primary School Children (F=4.939742, P=Sig.)

Table-12

(i) Means of Multifactor emotional intelligence scale of Primary School Children of Mass Media and Gender Status group

		Multifactor emotional intelligence scale	
		Mean	N
Internet	Boys	466.17	18
	Girls	499.28	142
	Total	495.56	160
TV	Boys	428.45	142
	Girls	463.00	18
	Total	432.34	160
Total	Internet	432.69	160
	TV	495.20	160
	Total	463.95	320

Table-12(a)

(ii) 2x2 analysis of variance of multifactor emotional intelligence scale of primary school children of mass media and gender Status group

Source of Variation	Sum of Squares	Df	Mean Square	F	Sig.
Mass Media (Internet & TV)	319728.8	1	319728.8	51.779	Sig.
Gender (Boys & Girls)	36570.45	1	36570.45	5.92246	Sig
2-Way Interaction Mass Media (Internet & TV) & gender Boys & Girls)	16.43138	1	16.43138	0.002661	N.S.
Residual	1951260	316	6174.875		
Total	2307576	319	7233.781		

* Significant at .05 level 'F' value at .05, (1,316)= 3.87

Table -12(a) pertaining to Multifactor emotional intelligence scale of Primary School Children response of total sample reveals that:-

i. There is significant effect of Multifactor emotional intelligence scale on of Social skills checklist of Primary School Children (F=51.779,P=Sig.)

ii. There is significant effect of Gender on Multifactor emotional intelligence scale of Primary School Children (F=5.92246,P=Sig.)

iii. There is no significant effect of Mass media and Gender group on Multifactor emotional intelligence scale of Primary School Children (F=0.002661,P=N.S.).

Table -13

(i) Means of **Cognitive capabilities test** of Primary School Children of Gender and Domicile Status group

	Cat	Cognitive capabilities test	
		Mean	N
1Boys	Rural	85.23	115
	Urban	86.71	45
	Total	85.65	160
2-Girls	Rural	73.42	45
	Urban	81.67	115
	Total	79.35	160
Total	Rural	81.91	160
	Urban	83.09	160
	Total	82.50	320

Table-13(a)

(ii) 2x2 Analysis of Variance of Cognitive capabilities test of Primary School Children of Gender and Domicile Status group

Source of Variation	Sum of Squares	Df	Mean Square	F	Sig.
Gender (Boys and Girls)	3175.2	1	3175.2	14.44429**	Sig
Domicile (Rural and Urban group)	1529.047	1	1529.047	6.955786**	Sig
2-Way Interaction Mass Media (Internet & TV) & Domicile (Rural & Urban)	741.4261	1	741.4261	3.37282	N.S.
Residual	69464.33	316	219.8238		
Total	74910	319	234.8276		

* Significant at .05 level 'F' value at .05, (1,316)= 3.87

Table -13(a) pertaining to Cognitive capabilities test of Primary School Children response of total sample reveals that:-

i. There is significant effect of Gender on Cognitive capabilities test of Primary School Children (F=14.44429,P=S.)

ii. There is significant effect of Domicile on Cognitive capabilities test of Primary School Children (F=6.955786,P=Sig.)

iii. There is no significant effect of Gender and Domicile on Cognitive capabilities test of Primary School Children (F=3.37282,P=N.S.).

Table -14

(i) Means of Social skills checklist of Primary School Children of Gender and Domicile Status group

		Social skills checklist	
	Cat	Mean	N
		99.57	115
1Boys	Rural	97.98	45
	Urban	99.13	160
	Total	99.91	45
2-Girls	Rural	103.96	115
	Urban	102.82	160
	Total	99.67	160
Total	Rural	102.28	160
	Urban	100.97	320
	Total	99.57	115

Table-14(a)

(ii) 2x2 Analysis of Variance of Social skills checklist of Primary School Children of Gender and Domicile Status group

Source of Variation	Sum of Squares	df	Mean Square	F	Sig.
Gender (Boys and Girls)	1091.503	1	1091.503	7.015668**	Sig
Domicile (Rural and Urban group)	97.01427	1	97.01427	0.623562	N.S.
2-Way Interaction Mass Media (Internet & TV) & Domicile (Rural & Urban)	514.7029	1	514.7029	3.938268*	Sig
Residual	49163.53	316	155.5808		
Total	50866.75	319	159.4569		

* Significant at .05 level 'F' value at .05, (1,316)= 3.87

Table 14(a) pertaining to Social skills checklist of Primary School Children response of total sample reveals that:-

I. There is significant effect of Gender on Social skills checklist of Primary School Children (F=7.015668,P=Sig.)

II. There is no significant effect of Domicile on Social skills checklist of Primary School Children (F=0.623562,P=N.S.)

III. There is significant effect of Gender and Domicile on Social skills checklist of Primary School Children (F=3.938268,P=Sig.).

Table 15

(i) Means of Multifactor Emotional Intelligence scale of Primary School Children of Gender and Domicile Status group

	Cat	Multifactor Emotional Intelligence scale	
		Mean	N
1Boys	Rural	436.30	115
	Urban	423.49	45
	Total	432.69	160
2-Girls	Rural	518.49	45
	Urban	486.09	115
	Total	495.20	160
Total	Rural	459.41	160
	Urban	468.48	160
	Total	463.95	320

Table-15(a)

(ii) 2x2 Analysis of Variance of Multifactor Emotional Intelligence scale of Primary School Children of Gender and Domicile Status group

Source of Variation	Sum of Squares	df	Mean Square	F	Sig.
Gender (Boys and Girls)	312562.5	1	312562.5	50.5022	Sig.
Domicile (Rural and Urban group)	33052.5	1	33052.5	5.340448	Sig
2-Way Interaction Mass Media (Internet & TV) & Domicile (Rural & Urban)	6209.525	1	6209.525	4.013302	Sig
Residual	1955752	316	6189.087		
Total	2307576	319	7233.781		

* Significant at .05 level 'F' value at .05, (1,316)= 3.87

Table 15.(a) pertaining to Multifactor emotional intelligence scale of Primary School Children response of total sample reveals that:-

i. There is significant effect of Gender Multifactor emotional intelligence scale of Primary School Children (F=50.5022,P=Sig.)

ii. There is significant effect of Domicile on Multifactor emotional intelligence scale of Primary School Children (F=5.340448,P=Sig.)

iii. There is significant effect of Gender and Domicile on Multifactor emotional intelligence scale of Primary School Children (F=4.013302,P=Sig.).

iv.

Table-16

(i) Means of Cognitive capabilities test on Primary School Children of Mass media and Domicile Status group

	Cat	Cognitive capabilities test	
		Mean	N
TV	Rural	76.98	53
	Urban	80.71	107
	Total	79.48	160
Internet	Rural	84.36	107
	Urban	87.89	53
	Total	85.53	160
Total	Rural	81.91	160
	Urban	83.09	160
	Total	82.50	320

Table-16(a)

(ii) 2x2 Analysis of Variance of Cognitive capabilities test of Primary School Children of Mass media and Domicile Status group

Source of Variation	Sum of Squares	Df	Mean Square	F	Sig.
Mass Media (Internet & TV)	2928.2	1	2928.2	13.0239 6	Sig
Domicile (Rural & Urban)	934.2835	1	934.283 5	4.15547 9	Sig
2-Way Interaction Mass Media (Internet & TV) & Domicile (Rural & Urban)	0.691236	1	0.69123 6	0.00307 4	N.S.
Residual	71046.83	316	224.831 7		
Total	74910	319	234.827 6		

* Significant at .05 level 'F' value at .05, (1,316)= 3.87

Table -16(a) pertaining to Cognitive capabilities test of Primary School Children response of total sample reveals that:-

iv. There is significant effect of Mass media on Cognitive capabilities test of Primary School Children (F=**13.02396**,P=S.)

v. There is significant effect of Domicile on Cognitive capabilities test of Primary School Children (F=**4.155479**,P=S.)

vi. There is no significant effect of Mass media and Domicile group on Cognitive capabilities test of Primary School Children (F=**0.003074**,P=N.S.).

Table-17

(i) Means of Social skills checklist of Primary School Children of Mass media and Domicile Status group

		Social skills checklist	
		Mean	N
TV	Rural	100.53	53
	Urban	102.45	107
	Total	101.81	160
Internet	Rural	99.24	107
	Urban	101.92	53
	Total	100.13	160
Total	Rural	99.67	160
	Urban	102.28	160
	Total	100.97	320

Table-17(a)

(ii) 2x2 Analysis of Variance of Social skills checklist of Primary School Children of Mass media and Domicile Status group

Source of Variation	Sum of Squares	Df	Mean Square	F	Sig.
Mass Media (Internet & TV)	226.1281	1	226.1281	1.421877	N.S.
Domicile (Rural & Urban)	375.2939	1	375.2939	2.35982	N.S.
2-2-Way Interaction Mass Media (Internet & TV) & Domicile (Rural & Urban)	10.26962	1	10.26962	0.064575	N.S.
Residual	50255.06	316	159.035		
Total	50866.75	319	159.4569		

* Significant at .05 level 'F' value at .05, (1,316)= 3.87

Table-17(a) pertaining to Social skills checklist of Primary School Children response of total sample reveals that:-

I. There is no significant effect of Mass media on Social skills checklist of Primary School Children (F=1.421877,P=N.S.)

II. There is no significant effect of Domicile Social skills checklist of Primary School Children (F=2.35982,P=N.S.)

III. There is no significant effect of Mass media and Domicile group on Social skills checklist of Primary School Children (F=0.064575,P=N.S.)

Table-18

(i) Means of Multifactor emotional intelligence scale of Primary School Children of Mass media and Domicile Status group

		Multifactor emotional intelligence scale	
		Mean	N
TV	Rural	509.02	53
	Urban	488.89	107
	Total	495.56	160
Internet	Rural	434.84	107
	Urban	427.28	53
	Total	432.34	160
Total	Rural	459.41	160
	Urban	468.48	160
	Total	463.95	320

Table-18(a)

(ii) 2x2 Analysis of Variance of multifactor emotional intelligence scale of Primary School Children of Mass media and Domicile Status group

Source of Variation	Sum of Squares	df	Mean Square	F	Sig.
Mass Media (Internet & TV)	319728. 8	1	319728. 8	51.2485	Sig
Domicile (Rural & Urban)	13587.1 4	1	13587.1 4	2.17784 7	N.S.
2-Way Interaction Mass Media (Internet & TV) & Domicile (Rural & Urban)	2801.44 2	1	2801.44 2	0.44903 6	N.S.
Residual	1971459	31 6	6238.79 3		
Total	2307576	31 9	7233.78 1		

* Significant at .05 level 'F' value at .05, (1,316)= 3.87

Table -18(a) pertaining Multifactor emotional intelligence scale of Primary School Children response of total sample reveals that:-

v. There is significant effect of Mass media on Multifactor emotional intelligence scale of Primary School Children (F=51.2485,P=S.)

vi. There is no significant effect of Domicile on Multifactor emotional intelligence scale of Primary School Children (F=2.177847,P=N.S.)

vii. There is no significant effect of Mass media and Multifactor emotional intelligence scale of Primary School Children (F=0.449036,P=N.S.).

<u>Abbreviations used in all the tables and figures :</u>

A – Mass Media	A_1 – TV
B – Gender	A2 – Internet
C – Domicile	B_1 – Boys
	B_2– Girls
	C_1 – Rural
	C_2 – Urban

Table –19

Means of **Cognitive capabilities test** of Primary School Children of Mass media, Gender group and Domicile Status group

FACTOR COMBINATION	Level-I	Level-II
A	79.48	85.53
B	73.42	79.35
C	81.91	83.09
AB : B_1	84.17	78.88
B_2	85.84	87.89
BC : C_1	76.98	80.71
C_2	84.36	83.06
AC : C_1	85.23	86.71
C_2	81.67	81.67
ABC : B_1C_1	81.93	75.03
B_1C_2	85.73	85.84
B_2C_1	95.33	80.29
B_2C_2	86.10	64.71
TOTAL	82.50	

Table-19(a)

(ii) 2x2x2 Analysis of Variance of **Cognitive capabilities test** of Primary School Children of Mass media, Gender and Domicile Status group

Source of Variation	Sum of Squares	Df	Mean Square	F	Sig.
Between Mass Media (TV Vs Internet)	2928.2	1	2928.2	13.77252	Sig
Between Gender (Boys Vs Girls)	520.0379	1	520.0379	2.445951	N.S
Between Domicile (Rural Vs Urban)	1525.508	1	1525.508	7.175088	Sig
Interaction Mass Media (TV Vs Internet) X Gender (Boys Vs Girls)	5.116195	1	5.116195	0.024064	N.S
Interaction Mass Media (TV Vs Internet) X Domicile (Rural Vs Urban)	633.63	1	633.63	2.980221	N.S
Interaction Gender (Boys Vs Girls)X Domicile (Rural Vs Urban)	1407.447	1	1407.447	6.619801	Sig
Interaction Mass Media (TV Vs Internet) X Gender (Boys Vs Girls) X Domicile (Rural Vs Urban)	2029.478	1	2029.478	9.545466	Sig.
Residual	66334.86	312	212.6117		
Total	74910	319	234.8276		

Table 19(a) pertaining to Cognitive capabilities test of Primary School Children response of total sample reveals that:-

1. There is significant effect of Mass Media on Cognitive capabilities test of Primary School Children (F=13.77252,P=S.)

2. There is no significant effect of Gender on Cognitive capabilities test of Primary School Children (F=2.445951, P=N.S.)
3. There is significant effect of Domicile on Cognitive capabilities test of Primary School Children (F=7.175088, P=Sig.)
4. There is no significant effect of Mass Media and Gender on Cognitive capabilities test of Primary School Children (F=0.024064,P=N.S.)
5. There is no significant effect of Mass Media and Domicile On Cognitive capabilities test of Primary School Children (F=2.980221,P=.N.S.)
6. There is significant effect of Gender and Domicile on Cognitive capabilities test of Primary School Children (F=6.619801, P=Sig.)
7. There is significant effect of Mass Media, Gender and Cognitive capabilities test of Primary School Children (F=9.545466, P=Sig.).

Table 20

(i) Means of Social skills checklist of Primary School Children of Mass media, Gender group and Domicile Status Group

FACTOR COMBINATION	Level-I	Level-II
A	101.81	100.13
B	99.13	102.82
C	99.67	102.28
AB : B_1	100.83	100.53
B_2	98.91	101.92
BC : C_1	100.53	102.45
C_2	99.24	109.78
AC : C_1	99.57	97.98
C_2	99.91	103.96
ABC : B_1C_1	100.80	100.42
B_1C_2	99.39	97.14
B_2C_1	101.00	101.94
B_2C_2	97.76	117.82
TOTAL	100.97	

Table-20(a)

(ii) 2x2x2 Analysis of Variance of Social skills checklist of Primary School Children of Mass media, Gender and Domicile Status Group

Source of Variation	Sum of Squares	Df	Mean Square	F	Sig.
Between Mass Media (TV Vs Internet)	226.1281	1	226.1281	1.510505	N.S
Between Gender (Boys Vs Girls)	1144.956	1	1144.956	7.648147	Sig
Between Domicile (Rural Vs Urban)	96.11144	1	96.11144	0.642011	N.S
Interaction Mass Media (TV Vs Internet) X Gender (Boys Vs Girls)	173.8181	1	173.8181	1.161081	N.S
Interaction Mass Media (TV Vs Internet) X Domicile (Rural Vs Urban)	697.7721	1	697.7721	4.661021	Sig
Interaction Gender (Boys Vs Girls)X Domicile (Rural Vs Urban)	1273.558	1	1273.558	8.507194	Sig
Interaction Mass Media (TV Vs Internet) X Gender (Boys Vs Girls) X Domicile (Rural Vs Urban)	593.5293	1	593.5293	3.964693	Sig
Residual	46707.56	312	149.7037		
Total	50866.75	319	159.4569		

Table 20(a) pertaining to Presentation Social skills checklist response of total sample reveals that:-

1. There is no significant effect of Mass Media on Social skills checklist of Primary School Children (F=1.510505,P=N.S.)

2 There is significant effect of Gender on Social skills checklist of Primary School Children (F=7.648147, P=S.)

3 There is no significant effect of Domicile on Social skills checklist of Primary School Children (F=0.642011,P=N.S.)

4 There is no significant effect of Mass Media and Gender on Social skills checklist of Primary School Children (F=1.161081,P=N.S.)

5. There is significant effect of Mass Media and Domicile On Social skills checklist of Primary School Children (F=4.661021,P=Sig.)

6. There is significant effect of Gender and Domicile on Social skills checklist of Primary School Children (F=8.507194, P=Sig.)

7 There is significant effect of Mass Media, Gender and Domicile on Social skills checklist of Primary School Children (**F**=3.964693, P=Sig.).

Table –21

Means of Multifactor emotional intelligence scale of Primary School Children of Mass media, Gender and Domicile Status Group

FACTOR COMBINATION	Level-I	Level-II
A	495.56	432.34
B	432.69	495.20
C	459.41	468.48
AB : B_1	466.17	499.28
B_2	428.45	427.28
BC : C_1	509.02	488.89
C_2	434.84	463.00
AC : C_1	436.30	423.49
C_2	518.49	486.09
ABC : B_1C_1	482.07	519.66
B_1C_2	429.43	512.14
B_2C_1	386.67	491.84
B_2C_2	426.12	431.73
TOTAL	463.95	

Table-21(a)

(ii) 2x2x2 Analysis of variance of multifactor emotional intelligence scale of primary school children of mass media, gender and Domicile Status

Source of Variation	Sum of Squares	Df	Mean Square	F	Sig.
Between Mass Media (TV Vs Internet)	319728.8	1	319728.8	53.09023	S
Between Gender (Boys Vs Girls)	36570.45	1	36570.45	6.072439	S
Between Domicile (Rural Vs Urban)	32844	1	32844	5.45367	S
Interaction Mass Media (TV Vs Internet) X Gender (Boys Vs Girls)	184.8869	1	184.8869	0.0307	N.S
Interaction Mass Media (TV Vs Internet) X Domicile (Rural Vs Urban)	49.58926	1	49.58926	0.008234	N.S
Interaction Gender (Boys Vs Girls)X Domicile (Rural Vs Urban)	2939.034	1	2939.034	0.48802	N.S
Interaction Mass Media (TV Vs Internet) X Gender (Boys Vs Girls) X Domicile (Rural Vs Urban)	29755.57	1	29755.57	4.940844	Sig
Residual	1878978	312	6022.366		
Total	2307576	319	7233.781		

Table 21(a) pertaining to Multifactor emotional intelligence scale of Primary School Children response of total sample reveals that:-

1. There is significant effect of Mass Media on Multifactor emotional intelligence scale of Primary School Children (F=53.09023,P=Sig.)

2. There is significant effect of Gender on multifactor emotional intelligence scale of Primary School Children (F=6.072439, P=Sig)
3. There is significant effect of Domicile on multifactor emotional intelligence scale of Primary School Children (F=**5.027677**,P=Sig)
4. There is no significant effect of Mass Media and Gender on multifactor emotional intelligence scale of Primary School Children (F=0.03072,P=N.S.)
5. There is no significant effect of Mass Media and Domicile On multifactor emotional intelligence scale of Primary School Children (F=0.008234,P=.N.S.)
6. There is no significant effect of Gender and Domicile on multifactor emotional intelligence scale of Primary School Children (F=0.48802, P=N.S.)
7 There is significant effect of Mass Media, Gender and Domicile on multifactor emotional intelligence scale of Primary School Children (**F**=4.940844, P=Sig).

Where S = $\sqrt{\frac{(N_1-1)\ V1+\ (N_2-1)\ V_2}{N_1+N_2-2}}$

Where S was combined standard deviation of two groups X_1 and X_2 means. N_1 and N_2 are number of subject for the respective group.
V_1 and V_2 are variances.

4. ANOVA

The two-way ANOVA compares the mean differences between groups that have been split on two independent variables (called factors). The primary purpose of a two-way ANOVA is to understand if there is an interaction between the two independent variables on the dependent variable. The interaction term in a two-way ANOVA informs you whether the effect of one of your independent variables on the dependent variable is the same for all values of your other independent variable (and vice versa).

The three-way ANOVA is used to determine if there is an interaction effect between three independent variables on a continuous dependent variable (i.e., if a three-way interaction exists). As such, it extends the two-way ANOVA, which is used to determine if such an interaction exists between just two independent variables (i.e., rather than three independent variables).

The observations was analyzed using mean, S.D. ,t test and ANOVA . The summary observation was presented vide table 1 to 21 infra:

Table-18(a)

(ii) 2x2 Analysis of Variance of multifactor emotional intelligence scale of Primary School Children of Mass media and Domicile Status group

Source of Variation	Sum of Squares	df	Mean Square	F	Sig.
Mass Media (Internet & TV)	319728.8	1	319728.8	51.2485	Sig
Domicile (Rural & Urban)	13587.14	1	13587.14	2.177847	N.S.
2-Way Interaction Mass Media (Internet & TV) & Domicile (Rural & Urban)	2801.442	1	2801.442	0.449036	N.S.
Residual	1971459	316	6238.793		
Total	2307576	319	7233.781		

* Significant at .05 level 'F' value at .05, (1,316)= 3.87

Table -18(a) pertaining Multifactor emotional intelligence scale of Primary School Children response of total sample reveals that:-

v. There is significant effect of Mass media on Multifactor emotional intelligence scale of Primary School Children (F=51.2485,P=S.)

vi. There is no significant effect of Domicile on Multifactor emotional intelligence scale of Primary School Children (F=2.177847,P=N.S.)

vii. There is no significant effect of Mass media and Multifactor emotional intelligence scale of Primary School Children (F=0.449036,P=N.S.).

<u>Abbreviations used in all the tables and figures :</u>

A – Mass Media	A_1 – TV
B – Gender	A2 – Internet
C – Domicile	B_1 – Boys
	B_2– Girls
	C_1 – Rural
	C_2 – Urban

CPSIA information can be obtained
at www.ICGtesting.com
Printed in the USA
BVHW032259010822
643527BV00013B/351

9 788137 095694